Forensic
Organizational
Consulting

Fundamentals of Consulting Psychology Book Series

Assessing CEOs and Senior Leaders: A Primer for Consultants
J. Ross Blankenship

Coaching Psychology: Catalyzing Excellence in Organizational Leadership
Vicki V. Vandaveer and Michael H. Frisch

Consulting Psychology in National Security Organizations
Laurie B. Moret and Carroll H. Greene III

Consulting to Technical Leaders, Teams, and Organizations: Building Leadership in STEM Environments
Joanie B. Connell

The Ethical Practice of Consulting Psychology
Rodney L. Lowman and Stewart E. Cooper

Forensic Organizational Consulting: The Role of Psychologists in Litigation Support
Jay M. Finkelman with Linda Gomberg

An Introduction to Consulting Psychology: Working With Individuals, Groups, and Organizations
Rodney L. Lowman

Learning Interventions for Consultants: Building the Talent That Drives Business
Manuel London and Thomas Diamante

Transcultural Competence: Navigating Cultural Differences in the Global Community
Jerry Glover and Harris L. Friedman

Using Feedback in Organizational Consulting
Jane Brodie Gregory and Paul E. Levy

APA FUNDAMENTALS OF CONSULTING PSYCHOLOGY

Forensic Organizational Consulting

THE ROLE OF PSYCHOLOGISTS IN LITIGATION SUPPORT

JAY M. FINKELMAN
with LINDA GOMBERG

AMERICAN PSYCHOLOGICAL ASSOCIATION

The opinions and statements published are the responsibility of the author, and such opinions and statements do not necessarily represent the policies of the American Psychological Association.

Published by
American Psychological Association
750 First Street, NE
Washington, DC 20002
https://www.apa.org

Order Department
https://www.apa.org/pubs/books
order@apa.org

In the U.K., Europe, Africa, and the Middle East, copies may be ordered from Eurospan
https://www.eurospanbookstore.com/apa
info@eurospangroup.com

Typeset in Minion by Circle Graphics, Inc., Reisterstown, MD

Printer: Gasch Printing, Odenton, MD
Cover Designer: Naylor Design, Washington, DC

Library of Congress Cataloging-in-Publication Data

Names: Finkelman, Jay M., author. | Gomberg, Linda, author.
Title: Forensic organizational consulting : the role of psychologists in
   litigation support / by Jay M. Finkelman and Linda Gomberg.
Description: Washington, DC : American Psychological Association, 2022. |
   Series: Fundamentals of consulting psychology book series | Includes
   bibliographical references and index.
Identifiers: LCCN 2021059077 (print) | LCCN 2021059078 (ebook) |
   ISBN 9781433840326 (paperback) | ISBN 9781433840333 (ebook)
Subjects: LCSH: Forensic psychology.
Classification: LCC RA1148 .F485 2022 (print) | LCC RA1148 (ebook) |
   DDC 614/.15--dc23/eng/20211205
LC record available at https://lccn.loc.gov/2021059077
LC ebook record available at https://lccn.loc.gov/2021059078

https://doi.org/10.1037/0000295-000

Printed in the United States of America

10 9 8 7 6 5 4 3 2 1

This book is dedicated in loving memory of Florence and Milton Finkelman, who prepared and guided me through every aspect of growth, always emphasizing ethical behavior and professional achievement.

It is also dedicated to my incredibly wise, loving, and supportive wife, Princess Maria; our daughter, Jr. Princess Lauren; and our faithful German Shepherd-Belgian Malinois, RiRi—all of whom furnished the inspiration and support to complete this project.

Contents

Series Editor's Foreword

Rodney L. Lowman

The field of consulting psychology has blossomed in recent years. It covers the applications of psychology in consultation to organizations and systems, as well as at the individual and team levels. Unfortunately, there are very few graduate training programs in this field of specialization, so consulting psychology roles are mostly populated by those who came to consulting psychology after having trained in other areas of psychology—including industrial and organizational (I/O), clinical/counseling, and school psychology, among others. Yet such training is rarely focused on consulting psychology, and psychologists and graduate students, therefore, have to learn the needed skills through on-the-job training, reading books and articles, attending conferences and workshops, and being mentored in the foundational competencies of the field as they seek to transition into it.

After a number of years of editing *Consulting Psychology Journal: Practice and Research*, the field's flagship journal, I felt that an additional type of educational product was needed to help those transitioning into consulting psychology. The Society of Consulting Psychology, therefore, partnered with the American Psychological Association (APA) to develop a new book series. The idea was to create a series of monographs on specific foundational skill sets needed to practice in this area of specialization. Working with an editorial advisory board, consisting of Drs. Judith Blanton, Brodie Gregory, Skipton Leonard, myself (and initially Dale Fuqua and the late Edward Pavur, Jr.), our goal in the series has been to identify the major competencies needed by consulting psychologists and then to work with highly experienced authors to create short, accessible, but evidence-based texts that would be useful both as stand-alone volumes and in combination with one another. The readers would be graduate students in relevant training programs, psychologists planning a transition into consulting psychology, and practicing professionals who want to add to their areas of expertise.

What are the fundamental skills needed in consulting psychology practice? The following three sources provide useful starting points:

- *Guidelines for Education and Training at the Doctoral and Postdoctoral Level in Consulting Psychology (CP)/Organizational Consulting Psychology (OCP)*, created by the Society of Consulting Psychology and approved by the American Psychological Association in 2017 (Gullette et al., 2019);
- *Handbook of Organizational Consulting Psychology* (Lowman, 2002); and
- *An Introduction to Consulting Psychology: Working With Individuals, Groups, and Organizations* (Lowman, 2016).

Each of these contributions was organized around the concept of levels (individual, group, and organizational) as a taxonomy for identifying fundamental skills. Within and across each of those categories, two broad skill sets are needed: assessment and intervention.

As with many areas of psychological practice, the foundational skills that apply in one area may overlap into others in the taxonomy. Interventions with individuals, as in executive coaching, for instance, usually take place in the context of work with a specific team and within specific organizations, which themselves also constitute a type of "client" (Schein, 1999).

Understanding the systemwide issues and dynamics at the organizational level usually also involves consulting activities with specific executives and teams, and multicultural/international issues suffuse many of our roles. The APA Guidelines (Gullette et al., 2019) and the *Handbook* (Lowman, 2016) concluded, properly, that consulting psychologists need to be trained in and have, at least, foundational skills and experience at the individual, group, and organizational levels, even if they primarily specialize in one of these areas.

In inviting you to learn more about consulting psychology through this book series, I hope you will come to agree that this is an exciting and inherently interesting area of study, research, and professional practice. The series aims not just to cover relevant literature on specific topics in consulting psychology, but it also aims to capture the richness of this work by including case material that illustrates its applications. Readers will soon understand that consulting psychologists are real-world activists, energized by the opportunity to work in, and to have positive impact on, real-world environments.

Finally, as one who trained and practiced in both I/O and clinical psychology, I should note that consulting psychology has been the one area in which I felt that all of my training and skill sets were both welcomed and needed. And in a world where organizations and the individuals and teams within them greatly need help in functioning ethically and effectively, in bridging individual-, group-, and organization-level needs and constituencies, and in coping with the rapid expansion of knowledge and escalating competition and internationalization, this book series aims to make a difference by helping more psychologists join the ranks of qualified consulting psychologists. Collectively, we can have positive impact, not just on an area of specialization in psychology, but also the world.

ABOUT THIS BOOK

Traditionally trained I/O psychologists, such as the author of this book and the book series editor, were likely not to have studied forensic consultation or expert witness testimony as part of their graduate training. However, even those who may not choose to work primarily in forensic applications may well have opportunities to consult as expert witnesses on legal cases, especially in highly litigious areas. Indeed, lawsuits abound in certain personnel selection contexts, especially in the public sector (Jacobs & Denning, 2017). For example, a colleague once described consulting to a firefighter selection project for a major U.S. city. The project, she stated, was guaranteed from the outset to generate appeals, grievances, and lawsuits. In fact, before the names of the successful applicants had even been announced, attorneys were already advertising for participants to sign up to be part of a class-action lawsuit contesting the selection process and its results.

Forensic Organizational Consulting was written for psychologists and those in training to become psychologists, for those who are interested in learning more about forensic consultation. It is also relevant for those in other professions, including law students and attorneys.

Some psychologists, like Dr. Finkelman, have chosen to make forensic consultation and expert-witness testimony a major part of their professional practice. Others will only have a few such engagements over their careers. For those new to this type of consulting, there is much to learn from Dr. Finkelman's extensive forensic consulting psychology experience. Readers will also benefit from the book's many case examples that help this practice area come alive.

With the assistance of his attorney-colleague, Linda Gomberg, Dr. Finkelman presents a thorough introduction to this often-intimidating arena. Whether consulting on jury selection, testing litigation, fashioning alternative ways to present information and messages to a jury, or in providing expert-witness testimony, this book has something to offer. It also will help readers understand how the contexts and settings in which forensic services are provided differ from those in which psychological services are often delivered. The world of the law and of attorneys, versus that of psychologists, can differ sharply in expectations, expected or required behavior, and in the predominant cultures. Those new to this type of work will certainly benefit from this field guide.

Despite these differences, readers may be surprised to learn how intellectually stimulating and lucrative this kind of consultation can be. *Forensic Organizational Consulting* provides a valuable and accessible introduction to an expanding area of consulting psychology practice.

REFERENCES

Gullette, E. C. D., Fennig, J., Reynolds, T., Humphrey, C., Kinser, M., & Doverspike, D. (2019). Guidelines for education and training at the doctoral and postdoctoral levels in consulting psychology/organizational consulting psychology: Executive summary of the 2017 revision. *American Psychologist*, *74*(5), 608–614. https://doi.org/10.1037/amp0000462

Jacobs, R., & Denning, D. L. (2017). Public sector employment. In J. L. Farr & N. Tippins (Eds.), *Handbook of employee selection* (2nd ed., pp. 722–737). Psychology Press.

Lowman, R. L. (Ed.). (2002). *Handbook of organizational consulting psychology. A comprehensive guide to theories, skills, and techniques.* Jossey-Bass.

Lowman, R. L. (2016). *An introduction to consulting psychology: Working with individuals, groups, and organizations.* American Psychological Association. https://doi.org/10.1037/14853-000

Schein, E. H. (1999). *Process consultation revisited: Building the helping relationship.* Addison-Wesley.

Preface

I never expected in graduate school to become a forensic consulting psychologist, but over 450 case consultations, hundreds of sworn depositions as an expert witness and giving testimony, and 62 trials later, that is what I have integrated with my teaching and line-management positions. How I got into the field was rather accidental: A state's attorney for the New York State Human Rights Commission approached the chair of the Psychology Department of the Bernard M. Baruch College, The City University of New York, to ask for a recommendation of a professor with an industrial psychology background who would be willing to testify on behalf of the state in a discrimination lawsuit. The department chair suggested me, and I was ultimately designated as the state's expert witness in human resources (HR), testifying in New York State Supreme Court— as my first case. It was a very exciting experience, and I was hooked for life.

Hopefully, other psychologists will be sufficiently intrigued by the content and vignettes presented in this book to consider similar career paths. We explore the varied options that psychologists have within our legal system, both as testifying experts and as litigation consultants. The book is targeted to forensic consulting psychologists (FCPs), industrial and organizational psychologists, and forensic psychologists. It takes readers through the legal process and describes the opportunities that abound for those who are confident and willing to interact with the legal community and the jury system. This can be a great way to apply consulting skills in a direction not previously considered.

I derive deep satisfaction from teaching, but I cannot imagine anything more exhilarating than participating in litigation as an expert or as a consultant. Expert testimony is a form of teaching, although rather than being directed at traditional students, the focus shifts to educating a jury about areas of your expertise, which in my case is HR policy and fair employment practices. Litigation consulting is a form of teaching as well, the focus being to give the attorneys or the court itself a rich learning experience. And we are not limited to courtroom trials. As the book describes, our services have great utility in the increasingly popular alternate dispute resolution domain, including mediation and arbitration, as well as in bench trials that do not entail empaneling a jury.

The book highlights the challenges and rewards that are derived from providing these services, as well as some of the ethical implications for psychologists. (In fact, the reader may notice some vagaries in vignettes portraying actual case participation. This is purposeful in that ethics and some nondisclosure agreements require a certain amount of confidentiality.) Ways that psychologists can contribute to litigation and add value to the court system are identified. An added advantage for psychologists is that expert testimony and litigation consulting can easily be combined with other professional responsibilities, such as teaching and/or management. For professors, sharing the courtroom experience with students increases their understanding of what trials are like; for managers, greater familiarity with the litigation process can increase effectiveness in dealing with toxic individuals and/or assuming risk management responsibilities within their organizations.

Some FCPs will make litigation-related activities their primary vocational focus, either as sole practitioners or as principals (or founders) of a litigation consulting company, which may also elect to provide expert witness services. Many FCPs are doing exactly that. Career opportunities are more extensive as litigation becomes more ubiquitous in our society—and it is unlikely that trend will change anytime soon. FCPs provide a valuable service and are well compensated for their efforts. I anticipate you will appreciate the experience, make new discoveries, and gain fresh insights throughout the book. Enjoy the trip!

The first chapter introduces the variety of activities in which the FCP may participate. It introduces several central issues, including abuses in litigation and the general role of a psychologist in the legal system, and provides background information that might not be part of the FCP's actual job but does represent some realities of working in the courts.

The second chapter provides an overview of the science and art of expert testimony, including the reliability and scientific foundation of such testimony. The misguided characterization of human resources management (HRM) as "junk science" is disputed. Juror perception of expert witnesses is also considered, as is scientific jury selection and trial consulting. The discipline of human factors and ergonomics is explained.

The third chapter explores the jury trial process, in both civil and criminal trials, and how juries make decisions and render verdicts. The roles of emotions, media exposure, and witness attractiveness are explained. The utility of using standardized documents, such as the Pretrial Juror Attitude Questionnaire, is discussed. Also covered is voir dire, its definition, and its relationship to juror bias and decision making. The related and controversial role of peremptory challenges is addressed.

The fourth chapter is focused on the various tools of the forensic trade, including mock juries, shadow juries, focus groups, voir dire, and juror selection. The issue of jury selection bias is addressed. The critical role of the *Daubert* test is explained as it relates to consulting psychologists. Witness preparation and the development of opening statements and closing arguments are explored from the perspective of the FCP.

The fifth chapter explains the mystery of posttrial consultation, story-mediated models in civil litigation, and the prediction of jury verdicts. Special issues surrounding the perception of employment discrimination and HRM are considered. The qualities of an effective expert, as well as the ethical issues that may be encountered, are described. The psychology of litigation, damage awards, and propensity for risk are presented. The role of cognitive social psychology in employment discrimination law is discussed. The chapter concludes with an intriguing overview of the never-ending lie detection controversy.

The sixth and final chapter provides an overview of the exciting opportunities and challenges for consulting psychologists in litigation; an in-depth exploration of the ethics and legality of jury trial consulting is also considered. No book about the law and psychology would be complete in the 21st century without a discussion about and reference to technology, including the internet and social media. The roles of politics, race in jury selection, and litigation crowdfunding are reviewed, and online jury selection is considered.

Acknowledgments

The author gratefully acknowledges the extraordinary contributions to this manuscript by Dr. Linda Gomberg, JD, who worked with me for more than 3 years to enhance, refine, and rigorously document this book.

I wish to recognize the mentorship, friendship, and opportunities offered by Dr. Rodney Lowman, the series editor for this volume, who invited me to return to academia over 2 decades ago and subsequently provided multiple opportunities for scholarship and publication, culminating in this book. His tireless editing, feedback, and seemingly unending demands significantly enhanced the quality of the product.

My esteemed colleagues and administrators throughout the Chicago School of Professional Psychology provided inspiration, encouragement, and support throughout the years I worked on this project, especially President Michele Nealon, Chief Academic Officer Ted Scholz, Dean Danielle Sperandeo, and cherished friends in the Business Psychology department for Southern California (my second family) and at our campuses in Chicago, Washington, DC, and Dallas.

Finally, the many gifted and dedicated plaintiff and defense attorneys throughout the country with whom I've worked during the last 4 decades facilitated my understanding of the connection between human resources management employment practices and the intricacies of the civil litigation process.

Forensic Organizational Consulting

1

Overview of Forensic Consulting Psychology

The corporate defendant was being sued for wrongful death and products liability—a young child had suffocated in a motor vehicle. At stake in multiple civil actions, by multiple plaintiffs throughout the United States, was multimillions of dollars. This was the first case, and if it were decided in plaintiffs' favor, the defendant was certain that future litigation on these issues would not go well for the corporation. For this reason, the corporation and its attorneys decided that any expenses incurred in defending this initial litigation would be money well spent in protecting the business and its shareholders. Recommendations and any other advice would necessarily be strictly followed. To be assured that such recommendations could be trusted, the defendant hired a well-known team of attorneys and other consultants, including forensic consulting psychologists (FCPs), to investigate and advise.

https://doi.org/10.1037/0000295-001
Forensic Organizational Consulting: The Role of Psychologists in Litigation Support, by J. M. Finkelman with L. Gomberg

Although the primary consulting team was recruited from the Los Angeles area, the venue (actual court location) was a large island territory that could not be reached via direct flights from the mainland. The morning after arriving on the island, the visiting team met with local attorneys engaged by the defendant's insurance carrier. This meeting is common practice for at least a couple of reasons. First, potential jurors may have implicit biases against "big city" litigators and may see them as "hired guns" defending the "deep pockets" of their client. More practically, though, the out-of-state attorneys may have licensure issues if they appear in court without local sponsors.

Next, the defense team attended a prearranged meeting with the marketing department at a local university. The department was chosen both for its experience in recruiting focus groups that mirrored the population in that trial venue and its research skills in identifying and surveying stratified random samples for their more typical advertising projects. After asking them to sign Confidentiality and Nondisclosure Agreements, we quickly brought the group members up to speed on the object of our litigation research, while at the same time providing them with only the essential facts at issue.

The marketing professors did their job well, and within 2 days identified and recruited multiple focus groups that accurately mirrored the likely composition of a potential jury. The evening before the first focus group was scheduled to begin, the consulting team, now consisting of FCPs, reviewed the final strategy and approach with the defense attorneys.

The death of a child makes for a particularly egregious case, and the focus groups consistently demonstrated a propensity for awarding in excess of a $10,000,000 liability verdict, plus substantial punitive damages and attorney's fees. That evening, the litigators and our team of FCPs contacted the insurance carrier with the focus group and survey results. Our strong recommendation was to settle the case and avoid trial at all costs, because it became apparent that juries in that venue would be very sympathetic to the plaintiff, given the horrendous facts in the case.

The defense attorneys and the insurance carrier agreed—it was too dangerous to the corporation to try the case. With prior approval from the presiding judge, the trial was put on hold, and settlement negotiations began within a few days. Although experience put the final settlement in the many millions of dollars, the exact amount was sealed, and it was never revealed to our team.[1]

Although the reader may question the moral and ethical issues inherent in advising a corporation to save money when the death of a child is at issue, the ethics and practicality of the actual case must also be considered: The client was the defendant, and the team was being paid by the corporate defendant. It is the job of the attorney to be an advocate for the client and the job of the FCP to be a neutral evaluator based on the facts of the case. Therefore, the attorneys were duty-bound to try to keep costs as low as possible for the client. The job of the FCP, of course, was to evaluate the facts of the situation based on the evidence accumulated. By deciding against a trial and offering a settlement, the defendant/client would be acknowledging that the plaintiff deserved compensation, and the exorbitant court costs of a trial would be avoided. In other words, this could be a true "win/win" result for all involved.

TYPES OF FORENSIC CONSULTING PSYCHOLOGY ACTIVITIES

The various books in this series reveal and confirm that consulting psychology takes many forms and creates many potential roles and client types for the consulting psychologist. As this case illustrates, however, no matter what the specific client need is, the FCP has one overarching role: The FCP has been hired by the legal professional or litigant for a legal purpose, to provide psychological expertise within and through the court or courts. Therefore, the FCP may be hired to participate in jury selection and witness preparation, as well as to organize mock trials and focus groups, provide expert testimony and psychological evaluation, or even to conduct change of venue surveys. Because a "legal purpose" may or may not involve actual litigation, the FCP's role, as was seen in the

---

[1]This might be an appropriate time to note that all references to personal/professional experiences are those of the first author.

original case, may or may not include participation in a trial. So, although this first chapter provides an overview of the entire field of forensic consulting psychology, this book is written with the intent to take the future or current FCP reader through that nonlinear path while taking whatever relevant detours present themselves along the way. Specifically, as the vignette demonstrated, from the inception of the hire, the FCP must be aware of the role(s) they are being asked to take in the process.

For that reason, the remainder of the book will more specifically address the major contributions psychologists make in forensic consulting psychology. It also reviews the relevant literature and supporting evidence to assess the efficacy of the contributions of FCPs to clients, the courts, and the legal system in general. Relevant statutory and case law, as well as certain legal interpretations, are interjected throughout, with particular attention to the Federal Rules of Evidence (FRE; 2021) and the resulting decision in *Daubert v. Merrell Dow Pharmaceuticals, Inc.* (1993).

Although the specifics of the case that opened this chapter may be unique to the facts of that litigation, the process utilized by the litigation support team in the case example was typical and illustrates what FCPs (the generic term used in this book) are frequently expected to contribute when retained. The purpose of this book is to give a clearer, broader picture of the range of related activities in which the consulting forensic psychologist participates in legal matters. These activities not only include trials and trial preparation; they also include the entire process of participation in the case—from retention by the parties, through discovery, trial, settlement, dismissal, or any other final resolution.

To that end, this book addresses the ever-expanding professional activities of the FCP. Some of those activities are more complex and play a larger part in the FCP's career; those activities are deserving of their own chapter, while others are woven throughout the various references and experiences. Their professional activities are included next.

Working With Witnesses

Working with different types of witnesses—from eyewitnesses to fact-based witnesses to expert witnesses—is integral to forensic consulting. Courts recognize three different kinds of witnesses: fact, eye, and expert (Gomberg, 2018). A *fact* witness may be law enforcement, a coroner, statistician, or another person with factual knowledge who can relate objective information about the facts of a given case. *Eyewitnesses* have relevant information, because they were there at the time the cause of action arose or, in some instances, they can provide factual background information. *Experts* may or may not have knowledge or opinions specific to the facts of a case, but they do have expertise in a topic or issue relevant to the matter being tried (*Daubert v. Merrell Dow Pharmaceuticals, Inc.*, 1993; FRE 702, 2021).

Admissibility of expert testimony has a long and still-evolving legal foundation and is discussed in detail in Chapter 2. However, the admissibility of testimony by any of these types of witnesses is dependent on its relevance to helping resolve the issues before the court (FRE 402, 2021). Further, among other conditions, the probative value of that relevant evidence must not be outweighed by its prejudicial effect on the finder of fact, which is most often the jury (FRE 403, 2021). Ultimately, upon motion by either party, it is the trial judge who decides if the evidence is relevant and if its probative value does or does not outweigh its prejudicial effect (see Chapter 2).

The FCP's job in working with witnesses of whatever type begins as soon as the attorney begins putting the potential case together. Who will be testifying? What is their role? How will they present to a judge and/or jury? Given media portrayals of unscrupulous attorneys, jury tampering, witness threatening, and other dramatic interference with the litigation process, novice and future consultants might have some concern about the common trial practice of witness preparation. The apprehension is heightened by the anticipated effectiveness of witness preparation in enhancing critical testimony delivery skills. This might not be an issue if there was reason to believe that all parties to litigation were in a comparable financial position to avail themselves equally of professional witness preparation. But that is rarely the case. Of course, attorneys can assume some preparation responsibility for their own witnesses, but litigators may not be equally proficient in imparting these skills, even if they have and utilize them in the courtroom themselves.

Expert Reports and Witness Testimony

Expert reports and expert witness testimony can be required before or during an actual trial. This function deserves its own chapter, the reasons for which will become very clear in Chapter 2; however, all types of witnesses often need the expert guidance of the FCP.

Assessment of Individual Jurors

The assessment of individual jurors as to their predisposition and/or bias with respect to various case theories and arguments can be beneficial before, during, and after a trial. As discussed extensively in Chapters 3, 4, and 5, FCPs have a role in developing and reviewing potential juror questionnaires, observing potential juror behavior during voir dire (i.e., a common practice of attorney and/or judge questioning of potential jurors prior to empaneling them), assessing those potential and seated juror responses to questions and evidence presentation, and even interviewing willing jurors postverdict/postjudgment.

The purpose of the posttrial interview is to gain insight into the decision process and rationale utilized by jurors during deliberation, which helps to inform future case strategy, including the selection of witnesses. Litigators are interested in juror perception, and the FCP is the logical professional to engage in this activity because their training prepares them for an informed interpretation of the reported behavior. Actual juror deliberations are held privately, however, and the right of confidentiality belongs to the individual juror.

Focus Group and Questionnaire Testing

Focus group and questionnaire testing of the differential impact of a range of opening and closing arguments, as well as trial tactics, serves the attorneys prior to the presentation of evidence and after all the evidence has been presented. Chapter 4 provides an extensive discussion of the various tools that FCPs have at their disposal to help understand the trial process, as well as to aid litigators (as discussed in Chapter 3). These tools include the above-mentioned questionnaires, shadow juries, focus groups, mock juries, and witness preparation.

Shadow juries consist of individuals resembling actual juror demographics; they actually sit in on evidence presentation and eventually come together to arrive at a possible verdict.

Focus groups are similarly made up of individuals with the same demographics as the jurors, but they do not participate in the trial. Prior to trial, they listen to presentations by litigators (or actors) from the side that recruited them in an effort to provide an assessment of the effectiveness of the potential opening statements.

Mock juries are recruited to listen to potential presentations by both sides and deliberate to a verdict. They are not present in the trial but hear presentations from both sides (actors usually replace attorneys for the opposing side, witnesses, and litigants).

In witness preparation, FCPs meet with and coach the various witnesses to help them present themselves in the best light for the trier of fact. In this context, coaching is limited to presentation style rather than content.

Anticipating Trial Outcomes

Empirically anticipating probable jury or bench trial outcomes before and even during litigation aids the litigants and their attorneys in understanding how and why they may want to settle, dismiss, or proceed to verdict in a case. The best example of this contribution was seen in the opening vignette. Because of the experience and expertise of the FCPs and litigation team, the client most likely avoided an eight-figure judgment. Although the advice derives from the entire litigation team, the FCP, as the most relevantly trained professional on the team, often takes the lead in integrating and distilling the recommendation to continue to or avoid trial. Within this process, the FCP also provides guidance regarding trial strategy and tactics.

Interviewing Willing Jurors Postverdict

Interviewing willing jurors after they have rendered a verdict helps litigation teams understand what worked and what failed in their case structure and presentation.

As stated above and discussed thoroughly in Chapter 5, contacting willing jurors after the fact is a significant role for the FCP. Again, just because one trial may be over, the FCP's job of understanding human nature in particular contexts does not end. The successful FCP continues to add to their skill sets regarding jurors and their thought processes in as many court contexts as possible. Insight regarding deliberation and decision-making processes will aid the FCP in future litigation matters.

Evaluation of Trial Venues and Courts

Evaluation of various trial venues and courts for their receptivity to the themes and theories of litigators on either side of both criminal and civil cases can often prevent costly mistakes for clients.

The trial *venue* is the actual court location of the litigation. An excellent example of poor venue selection comes to mind from an almost 3-decade-old case. In California, former football star and celebrity O. J. Simpson was tried for the murder of his former wife and her acquaintance, Ron Goldman. Although there was jurisdiction (the power of the court to hear and decide a case) anywhere within the County of Los Angeles, including the upscale portion of the county where the murders took place, the prosecutors chose downtown Los Angeles as the venue.

The prosecutors seemed so sure of a conviction that they chose a downtown venue, where there would be a more racially diverse jury. After an extremely well-publicized trial, Simpson was acquitted. Posttrial, there was speculation that the racial composition of the jury contributed to Simpson's acquittal. However, the criminal case was followed by a civil case wherein the plaintiffs were Simpson's children and Ron Goldman's heirs. For that case, the plaintiffs' chose to file their action in the court located in the upscale neighborhood where the victims were killed. The jury came back with a verdict against Simpson. Location, location, location!

TYPES OF LITIGATION

Very often, the type of litigation determines the type of FCP consultation that will be needed (i.e., the witnesses that will be called to testify as well as the type of preparation that is required). The American Bar Association (2020) defines *litigation* as the process by which contested legal disputes are handled by and through the courts. Although other matters find their way through the judicial system, and a few of those might require the testimony of witnesses (e.g., probate, contested family matters), generally, there are two major types of litigation: civil and criminal. Each of these processes is introduced and described.

Civil Litigation

Civil litigation involves a legal dispute between private parties. An individual/company/agency (i.e., the plaintiff) claims to have been harmed by another individual/company/agency (i.e., the defendant) and has the burden of proving that the defendant is liable. The liability, if found, is usually resolved by awarding monetary damages to the plaintiff (see Chapter 3). The most common types of civil litigation are in torts (i.e., civil wrongs committed against the plaintiff's person or property) and in breach of contract.

Two other points about civil litigation bear mentioning. In a civil lawsuit, the focus is on the plaintiff's perception of the defendant's action, and the burden on the plaintiff is to prove this to a preponderance of the evidence. An early 20th-century landlord–tenant case provides an excellent example. When a tenant was moving out of her apartment, the landlord pointed a gun at her and demanded that she leave her possessions, claiming she owed back rent. The tenant sued the landlord for assault, defined civilly as the intentional placing of another in fear of imminent danger (*Allen v. Hannaford,* 1926). The landlord's defense was that the gun was not loaded.

The court ruled that the landlord was liable because the plaintiff's perception of the defendant's intent was that she was in imminent danger.

The implication in looking at the civil burden of proof is that the role of the FCP may be even more crucial in determining or predicting a civil trial outcome, because the difference in perceived proof between winning or losing can be quite small (after all, how does one define a preponderance?) and the margin of error quite large. Incremental determinants of a verdict may be highly susceptible to trial strategy and tactics, in addition to witness preparation and coaching, when the outcome may be dependent on nuance or hundredths of a percentage point.

Greene (2003) explored the wide range of issues that are litigated in civil courts and are most likely to garner public attention, as well as in forensic psychology research. The author identified tort cases, including employment discrimination, sexual harassment, and personal injury disputes. Greene noted that focusing on tort cases omits many other areas of court filings that may entail substantive psychological issues, including wills, probate, family law, property law, and contract law.

Criminal Litigation

As stated previously, civil litigation involves private parties; *criminal* cases, however, involve acts against society, and they are punished to protect society. Therefore, the government prosecutes and has the burden of proving, beyond a reasonable doubt, that the defendant had both the requisite specific intent (i.e., guilty mind or *mens rea*) and committed the act (i.e., *actus reus*). In contrast to civil litigation, which focuses on the plaintiff's perception, criminal cases are viewed from the defendant's perspective. The question is whether the defendant had or could form the requisite intent to commit the crime. Although in civil litigation, a verdict for the plaintiff results in the defendant's liability to the plaintiff, in criminal litigation, a verdict for the prosecution results in the determination that the defendant committed the illegal act against society and results in suitable punishment.

In his review of Eisenberg's 2004 book, *Law, Psychology, and Death Penalty Litigation*, Goldstein (2005) reported that, in the case of *Wiggins v. Smith* (2003), the U.S. Supreme Court held that a capital defendant's

Sixth Amendment rights had been violated because defense counsel did not properly investigate the defendant's social history. According to Goldstein, Justice O'Connor reasoned that in order "to reach an informed decision as to whether or not to present mitigating evidence to a capital jury, counsel must investigate the defendant's history" (p. 123), in that this information could have influenced the jury's appraisal of culpability. The decision highlights the critical role that mental health professionals and FCPs are expected to play in both capital sentencing trials and in other criminal matters to help determine the defendant's intent (and ability to form it) beyond a reasonable doubt.

Mental health professionals may serve as trial consultants working with attorneys to prepare them to cross-examine opposing experts, to advise on jury selection, or to assist in the development of trial strategy. Other experts may offer testimony about a specific topic, such as battered spouse syndrome or the long-term effects of parental abuse and neglect on personality development (Eisenberg, 2005, p. 123).

The role of psychologists as trial consultants becomes even more crucial in death penalty litigation, not only because the stakes are so high but also because, as in all criminal cases, a higher standard of proof is required for conviction. The standard the prosecution must meet is beyond a reasonable doubt (see Chapter 5). Keeping in mind that the law doesn't define what is "reasonable," the need to persuade a jury becomes more challenging, and the utility of engaging FCPs at trial is more apparent.

In the remainder of this chapter, I address the following areas that compose the promised overview of forensic consulting psychology. What follows may not be thought of as actual "activities" of the FCP, but they are most definitely realities with which the FCP may have to contend. Under any conditions, the FCP needs to be aware and knowledgeable.

ABUSES OF LITIGATION

When there is money at stake, there is the foreseeable potential for fraud and misconduct. The legal system itself is not immune to this abuse but rather creates a tempting opportunity to exploit for dishonest litigants and possibly opportunistic attorneys motivated to do so. FCPs need to be aware of such abuses and take care not to support them.

Frivolous litigation, defined here as litigation with no basis in law or fact, has the potential to both overload and undermine the legal system unless it is detected and controlled. FCPs are educated in the signs of malingering and deception detection. The boundary between engaging in frivolous litigation, as opposed to low probability of success litigation, is highly subjective and situation specific.

Although not directly related to the focus of this book, a case from the litigious world of medical malpractice suits provides an overt example of frivolous litigation (R. M. Gomberg, personal communication, December 12, 2002). A day or so after the birth of a healthy baby boy, a pediatric nurse informed the pediatrician that the baby was dehydrated due to the mother's lack of milk production. The pediatrician explained to the mother that nursing would need to be supplemented with water or formula. The mother reacted angrily and threatened to sue the pediatrician for intentional infliction of emotional distress, a tort. The emotional distress inflicted, according to the mother, was that the doctor had "ruined" what should have been the happiest day of her life. Three hundred and sixty-four days later (the Statute of Limitations was 1 year), the suit was filed. The mother's suit was on behalf of her son, in case the child would eventually need mental health treatment due to being bottle fed for the first week of his life. As the mother was a law school graduate but not a licensed attorney, the suit was filed pro se (she acted as her own attorney). As "frivolous" as such a suit might seem, the plaintiff probably had good reason to believe she would collect. Insurance companies and other frequent defendants will often settle a case quickly to prevent further legal expenses. In this case, however, the malpractice insurance carrier threatened the plaintiff with an abuse of process suit, if she did not immediately move to voluntarily dismiss the action. Although she asked for a small settlement (which she did not get) to dismiss the suit, this frivolous filing did cause damage to the defendant, who was required to list the malpractice suit on hospital and credentialing applications for the next 10 years.

Guthrie (2000) offered a component of prospect theory to help understand the logic behind this type of litigation. Prospect theory explains that people respond differently to gains versus losses, and loss aversion typically is more compelling than the quest for gain—or winning in litigation. Prospect theory suggests that the decision frame in frivolous litigation is such that it triggers risk-aversive behavior in defendants and risk-seeking behavior in plaintiffs. "Because plaintiffs in frivolous litigation have a greater tolerance for risk than the defendants they have sued, plaintiffs in frivolous litigation have a psychological leverage in settlement negotiations, which is likely to lead to plaintiff-friendly settlements or bargaining impasse" (Guthrie, 2000, p. 163). Guthrie drew the logical conclusion that those concerned about frivolous litigation are best advised to target their reform efforts at the decision-making process of plaintiffs in frivolous lawsuits.

Although there is no justification for initiating frivolous litigation, it is not always possible for an attorney to discern the reality of the situation at the onset. Sometimes it only becomes apparent to the attorney representing a client after compelling exculpatory evidence is introduced by the defense. Additionally, attorneys want to believe their clients, are expected to be zealous advocates when they take a case, and admittedly may have financial incentives to accept a case. On the other hand, as mentioned at the beginning of this chapter, the FCP is neither an advocate nor an opponent and may be in position to help the attorney end the matter prior to expending unnecessary time and resources.

However, when it is the attorney who seeks and then initiates the frivolous lawsuit, as some attorneys did by soliciting clients to sue small businesses under the Americans With Disabilities Act (1990) throughout the State of California, the attorneys are subject to malicious prosecution liability, monetary sanctions, and even disbarment in egregious cases (*Hutchins v. Municipal Court*, 1976; *Molski v. Arby's Huntington Beach*, 2005).

Similarly, some plaintiffs believe they have been wronged, typically by an employer, and are easily persuaded by their own unfortunate circumstances to blame the employer for something out of their direct control. In some cases, employees are unwilling to accept their employer's adverse, but appropriate, performance-based action against them and may try to retaliate. Many workers are not entirely objective when it comes to their own performance and might prefer to blame someone else, typically the employer, for their deficiencies. It is easy and, for some employees quite satisfying, to initiate a lawsuit with a willing and often unknowing attorney, who is then obligated to be their advocate after agreeing to take the case.

In the more than 60 trials in which I've testified, there seems to be a discernible pattern in which discrimination lawsuits are triggered only after employees receive a less than stellar performance evaluation or are not promoted into positions they feel are deserved. But the biggest trigger for such litigation, in my experience, occurs when an actual termination takes place. Then an employee has little to lose by claiming the firing was in retaliation for having engaged in some protected activity, such as filing a complaint. And that may well be the case. But it is difficult for a third party to discern the reality without a thorough review of the personnel file and some level of investigation, depending on circumstances.

In the case of a dismissal, FCPs and human resources management professionals are likely to agree that the way in which the termination is conducted can have a significant impact on whether an employee elects to visit an attorney as the next stop after departing. For a variety of reasons, including but not limited to common decency, every effort should be made to allow a terminated employee to save face during the stressful exit interview and especially in front of colleagues still at work. The classic "perp walk," in which a fired employee is escorted out of a supervisor's office (or out of human resources), in front of everyone and often with security visibly present, is a textbook example of how not to terminate an employee for any reason—unless the intent is to trigger a lawsuit.

FORENSIC PSYCHOLOGISTS IN THE LEGAL SYSTEM

It seems fitting to close this introductory chapter with a brief consideration of the legal system climate—an environment that psychologists will find very different. Whereas FCPs' work in settings that are typically not adversarial (although they may be contentious at times), litigation consulting, even behind the scenes, is a departure from the norm. Attorney styles often differ from those of psychologists, and attorneys may go through more than one FCP before settling on the one or very few with whom they are comfortable working. In my experience, attorneys are more understanding of the role psychologists play in the legal system and the assistance they can provide for trial than the other way around. Psychologists are often unprepared for the noncollaborative nature of litigation and the inevitable win/lose outcomes. Even cases that settle are often extremely contentious throughout the negotiations.

Attorneys are required to be zealous advocates for their clients. Although television shows, such as *Law and Order*, often exaggerate the interactions among the parties for dramatic effect, those programs featuring criminal defense attorneys who tell their clients they do not care if they are guilty or not are fairly accurate. That is because if an attorney knows factually that a client is guilty, and the client pleads not guilty, the attorney cannot be the unbiased advocate legal ethics require. On the other hand, it deserves repeating that FCPs are required by professional ethics to be neutral parties, not "advocating" for one side or the other, except when the facts justify a particular point of view. FCPs, therefore, are independent fact finders and presenters, basing all opinions on valid and reliable evidence.

Nonetheless, testifying psychologists face a different type and level of scrutiny and sometimes outright hostility from opposing counsel. Sometimes the apparent hostility is an act, designed to intimidate or disparage a witness. But sometimes the hostility is an emotional reaction to an expert whose testimony may serve to undermine a case at the expense of a client for whom the attorney is advocating. Although trial judges are quite effective in minimizing, if not eliminating, angry outbursts in the presence of the jury, other parts of the case, for example, depositions (i.e., pretrial out-of-court testimony usually conducted in an attorney's office) are less regulated (even though depositions are always transcribed, often recorded with video, and sworn under penalty of perjury). There is nothing casual about depositions despite the fact that they take place outside the formality of a courtroom. The sworn testimony during a deposition can be and usually is played in court and/or read to the jury. The contributions of FCPs are essentially the same whether engaged in conjunction with depositions or courtroom testimony. The common element is the probable impact on and perception of trier(s) of fact, most often the jury.

Regardless of motive, to maintain credibility, testifying experts need to be able to maintain composure in court and not retreat from an opinion that is offered in good faith, given the facts and circumstances at hand. Experts need to expect that credentials, background, and professional experience may be severely challenged in attempts to undermine qualifications even before FCPs' expert testimony can be offered to the court. Once the expert does testify, the opposing counsel may aggressively cross-examine in an effort to try to impeach the opinions just offered to the jury. FCPs should anticipate being confronted with any prior testimony and/or their own published work. Experts can anticipate videos of their prior testimony being played to the jury, especially if there is an appearance of contradiction or inconsistency with current testimony.

If after several involvements with the legal environment, it is too far out of the comfort zone of FCPs, the solution is obvious: Do not go there. But above all, it is essential not to compromise professional standards or ethics, regardless of circumstances or pressure from either party to the litigation.

SUMMARY

In summary, this first chapter introduced the variety of activities in which the FCP may participate. A couple of issues were raised, including abuses in litigation and the general role of a psychologist in the legal system, which provided background information that might not be part of the FCP's actual job, but they do depict some realities of working in the courts. Seven of the activities were listed specifically and touched on as part of the overview. Expect to see them repeatedly throughout this book, as they exist independently and as integral parts of other consulting roles. As stated in that list, one of those activities, acting as an expert witness, has many components and is deserving of its own chapter (see Chapter 2).

2

Expert Witness Testimony

Forensic consulting psychologists (FCPs) may testify in and out of court (e.g., in depositions) as expert witnesses to assist triers of fact in coming to fair and just determinations in a variety of lawsuits requiring their specialized expertise. As mentioned in Chapter 1, one of the major roles of an FCP is to act as an expert witness in a given case. What follows in this chapter is the implicit definition, multifaceted history, and scientific foundation for that role, both in general and specifically to the FCP.

Drogin (2007) used the distinction between "probability" and "scientific certainty" as an example of the type of issue for which a forensic psychologist may add value by explaining the underlying scientific principles to a lay jury. FCPs can employ scientific analyses to examine the practice and domains of expert-witness work products. It is not unusual for FCPs to be called upon in a trial or deposition to differentiate between

https://doi.org/10.1037/0000295-002
Forensic Organizational Consulting: The Role of Psychologists in Litigation Support, by J. M. Finkelman with L. Gomberg

"correlation" and "causation" in psychometrics. An example would be litigation involving discrimination allegations with respect to assessment centers and employee-selection test batteries. Statistical analysis, in general, is a domain that may not be logical or intuitive to many juries, which can then benefit from a factually neutral presentation by qualified FCPs serving as expert witnesses. These are just two examples of how FCPs may find themselves delivering expert testimony; this and the remaining chapters implicitly and explicitly provide many more.

THE LAW AND EXPERT PSYCHOLOGICAL TESTIMONY

Legal constructs are not usually the same as psychological constructs. For example, the law defines insanity; although it seems to be a psychological term, psychology does not. Psychology never uses the term, but often psychologists are called upon to discuss the existence or nonexistence of the elements of the legal term (*Queen v. M'Naghten*, 1843; *Yates v. State of Texas*, 2005). Forensic consultants need to be aware of the legal approaches, to know some of the relevant content, and how these rules can affect the provision of psychological consultation.

Although psychologists have been experts in their focus of inquiry and practice for some time, it was not until 1962, in *Jenkins v. United States*, that the District of Columbia Circuit Court of Appeals agreed that psychologists are actually scientists whose professional opinions could be worthwhile additions in relevant court cases. In that case, the first of what, by 2019, had become 200 amicus curiae (literally "friend of the court") briefs was written and filed by the American Psychological Association (APA); the APA brief was accepted by the court as an authoritative statement regarding the scientific knowledge of doctoral-level psychologists (Bersoff, 2013; DeAngelis, 2019).

In the *Jenkins* case, Vincent Jenkins was accused of, and went on trial for, committing several criminal acts. Three psychologists had diagnosed him with schizophrenia; two of the three testified that the crimes were the product of the schizophrenia. Although the third psychologist gave no opinion as to causation, Jenkins's defense was insanity at the time of the commission of the crimes, a recognized defense in federal courts. However, the trial court's jury instructions included a statement that

> a psychologist is not competent to give a medical opinion as to a mental disease or defect. Therefore, you will not consider any evidence to the effect that the defendant was suffering from a mental disease or a mental defect on June 10, 1959, according to the testimony given by the psychologists. (*Jenkins v. United States*, 1962, p. 643)

To this statement the D.C. Appeals court responded, "The trial court apparently excluded these opinions because psychologists lack medical training. We agree with the weight of authority, however, that some psychologists are qualified to render expert testimony in the field of mental disorder" (*Jenkins v. United States*, 1962, p. 643).

Of course, this decision had its dissenters and much opposition from the American Psychiatric Association, the national organization of medically trained mental health doctors. The dissenters opposed the decision, using the "wise counsel" of the amicus curiae brief submitted by the American Psychiatric Association as their reference: "A clinical psychologist, lacking medical training and the specialization required of the qualified psychiatrist, is not qualified to make this total medical diagnosis or to testify as a medical expert thereon" (Amicus Curiae Brief for Appellant, *Jenkins v. United States*, 1962, p. 85).

So, in 1962, the federal courts recognized that the testimony of psychologists could be admissible as expert witnesses that "'could aid the trier in his search for truth'" (*Jenkins v. United States*, quoting McCormick on Evidence §13 [1955]). It was not until 1975, however, that the construct was codified in the Federal Rules of Evidence (FRE); the FRE was enacted for use in the federal courts. Most relevant to this discussion is FRE 702, entitled "Testimony by Expert Witnesses." The rule that lays the foundation for admissibility of expert testimony in federal courts, however, was not effectively utilized until 1993, when the U.S. Supreme Court decided *Daubert v. Merrell Dow Pharmaceuticals, Inc.*

THE LEGAL HISTORY OF ADMISSIBILITY
OF EXPERT TESTIMONY

In order to completely trace the legal history of admissibility of expert testimony in the United States, it is necessary to go back to 1923 (yes, the law moves slowly) and the case of *Frye v. United States*. As is the story with much case law that's relevant to specific topics (i.e., psychology), the cause of action in the original case was not the issue on appeal. The specific reason the case was appealed and then was reported by the D.C. Circuit Court was the admissibility of certain purported expert testimony.

Keeping in mind that the trier of fact can only consider testimony that the court deems admissible (no matter what the juror[s] may know from outside knowledge), Frye appealed his second-degree murder conviction based on the pretrial court's exclusion of what he considered exculpatory evidence—the testimony of a lie detector expert. The testimony that was excluded was the readout of what was then called the systolic blood pressure deception test or what is currently called a polygraph. The test was then and it remains today inadmissible in the courts. The statement in Frye was only that scientific testimony that is "sufficiently established to have gained general acceptance in the particular field in which it belongs" will be admitted as expert testimony (*Frye v. United States,* 1923). Then and now, the results of deception detection instruments, as a general rule, are not admitted as evidence into courts.

However, although that specific form of evidence is not admissible, the general acceptance standard, espoused in 1923, was eventually abandoned in federal courts. After 70 years, the U.S. Supreme Court accepted the case of *Daubert v. Merrell Dow Pharmaceuticals, Inc.* to rule on the same point regarding admissibility of expert scientific testimony. The 1993 case had no substantive or procedurally similar facts to those at issue in *Frye*. *Daubert* was a civil suit brought by children and their parents against a drug manufacturer, because the mothers had ingested its drug during pregnancy, and allegedly the children were born with significant defects. Before trial, the defendant moved for summary judgment (i.e., asserting that there were no arguable material issues of fact for trial), because the expert testimony proffered by the plaintiffs was excluded under *Frye*.

Defendant's expert had submitted testimony that the scientific community found no connection between the drug and the birth defects. In the lower court, the defendant's motion was granted, and the plaintiffs appealed to the U.S. Supreme Court based on one issue: Was it error to exclude the plaintiffs' expert(s) scientific testimony regarding the defendant's drug?

Eighteen years after the adoption of the Federal Rules of Evidence, and 70 years after the "*Frye* Standard" for admissibility was adopted, the U.S. Supreme Court stated in *Daubert* that the *Frye* "general acceptance" test was no longer the standard for admissibility of scientific evidence in the federal courts. Instead, Justice Harry Blackmun wrote that when a federal rule is on point, that rule will be utilized in decision making. Of course, the opinion was not quite that simplistic. First, the Court cited FRE 402, which, along with FRE 403, is recited in paraphrased parts by every first-year law student: All relevant evidence is admissible unless its probative value is outweighed by its prejudicial effect. Relevancy goes to its probability of usefulness in helping to determine the outcome (see FRE 401, 2021). Clearly, the expert testimony was relevant, but the Court looked to FRE 702 to judge the strength of the probative value. As such, the court indicated that a witness who is qualified as an expert by knowledge, skill, experience, training, or education may testify in the form of an opinion or otherwise if

- the expert's scientific, technical, or other specialized knowledge will help the trier of fact to understand the evidence or to determine a fact in issue;
- the testimony is based on sufficient facts or data;
- the testimony is the product of reliable principles and methods; and
- the expert has reliably applied the principles and methods to the facts of the case.

Although all nine justices agreed that the FRE should control the standard, two disagreed with the application set forth in the majority opinion. Justices Rehnquist and Stevens were uncomfortable that, in reversing the judgment and remanding the case to the lower court, the majority said the decision of admissibility would ultimately rest with the court in each case.

This, said the dissenters, asks too much of a judge. Judges are not scientists, and although FRE 702 probably does give trial judges some "gatekeeping responsibility," the majority decision also "imposes on them either the obligation or the authority to become amateur scientists in order to perform that role" (*Daubert v. Merrell Dow Pharmaceuticals, Inc.*, 1993, p. 601).

In 1999, the U.S. Supreme Court decided *Kumho Tire Co. v. Carmichael*, where not only was the Court's interpretation of the application of FRE 702 confirmed, after almost 4 decades, the decision seemed to bring the question of psychological expert testimony full circle.

Although one of the questions in *Jenkins v. United States* (1962) was whether doctoral-level psychologists are "scientists" qualified to testify as experts, the decision in *Kumho* held that FRE 702 was flexible enough to allow for the admissibility of testimony of nonscientists. Therefore, the issue of whether psychologists were scientists became moot as to the admissibility of their expert testimony, i.e., if their "opinion" was relevant and reliable (*Kumho Tire Co. v. Carmichael*, 1999). The one to make that determination, the "gatekeeper," is the trial judge (*Daubert v. Merrell Dow Pharmaceuticals, Inc.*, 1993; Schweitzer & Saks, 2009).

QUALIFICATIONS OF EXPERT WITNESSES AND THE ACCURACY AND INTEGRITY OF THEIR TESTIMONY

Kafadar (2017) highlighted what she considered to be some deficiencies in FRE 702 regarding the qualification of expert testimony and the assurance of a reliable scientific foundation for psychological testimony. The author maintained that experts should be obligated to identify the basis for their purported expertise and defend their methodology as valid and reliable. However, Kafadar argued that even qualified experts should not be permitted to testify about inferences they may have made based on the data. The concern is that experts should not express inferences as though they are factual, especially if they rely on methodology and statistics that may fall outside their demonstrated expertise and qualifications.

THE SCIENTIFIC FOUNDATIONS
OF FORENSIC TESTIMONY

In a 2005 work, Nielsen commented about a lawsuit in which I served as the plaintiff's expert witness, noting that California had formally enshrined the importance of human resources (HR) expert testimony as psychological testimony for employment litigation. On January 28, 2004, the days of industrial psychology or HR management being characterized as "junk science" in courtrooms abruptly ended with the California Court of Appeal's opinion in *Kotla v. Regents of University of California*. As of that date, persons with such expertise formally joined the ranks of recognized experts who may testify in litigation.

The Landmark *Kotla* Case

The First Appellate District Court of California held that "expert testimony on predicate issues within the expertise of a human resources expert is clearly permissible," confirming the legitimacy of expert testimony of qualified HR professionals in California courtrooms (*Kotla v. Regents of University of California*, p. 294, n. 6). The "junk science" testimony that the defendants alleged came from plaintiff's expert in the well-established discipline of industrial and organizational (I/O) psychology or human resource management (HRM; Nielsen, 2005). This is significant, because it provided precedent-setting acknowledgment (at least in California) of the scientific foundation on which it was based and, thus, the admissibility of forensic consulting psychology regarding generally accepted HRM policy and practice.

Nielsen (2005) concluded his article by stating, "After *Kotla*, human resources expert testimony on appropriate issues in employment cases will no longer be the object of derogatory 'common knowledge' or 'worse than junk science' references" (p. 164). During the years since the *Kotla* appellate court decision, Nielsen's prediction has proven to be accurate. Because I was the expert witness who apparently triggered the Appellate Court to overturn the verdict for plaintiff rendered by the trial court in that case, it is not surprising that opposing counsel will often bring up that decision without a full understanding of its implications (as articulated by Nielsen) almost every time I offer expert testimony.

When the *Daubert* decision came down in 1993, the new standard was limited to federal courts, and California (as well as many other states) did not completely adopt the *Daubert* Standard. Instead, although the California Evidence Code is similar to the FRE, the state courts seemed to remain on the cusp of the FRE and the *Frye* Standard.

The *Kotla* Court remanded the case for retrial, throwing out a seven-figure verdict in favor of the plaintiff. When the case was retried, and plaintiff's attorneys utilized the same expert witness, to the chagrin of defendants, the jury doubled the original damages award. That was not the extent of their problem. The often-quoted Footnote 6 of the Appellate Court decision referring to the testimony of this author, as quoted above, is instructive. It further reads in part: "Opinion testimony on these subjects by a qualified expert on human resources management might well assist the jury in its fact finding" (*Kotla v. Regents of University of California*, 2004, p. 294, n. 6).

The Abuse Defense in Sexual Harassment Litigation

"Junk logic" refers to the misapplication of ostensibly scientific principles to situations in which they do not necessarily apply. Using sexual harassment as an example, in marked contrast to the use of credible scientific evidence in other applications of HRM, Fitzgerald et al. (1999) took issue with the practice they attributed to some defense-oriented authorities; those defense-oriented authorities maintained that a history of childhood sexual abuse can be employed to undermine a wide variety of the elements of a sexual harassment victim's case. Fitzgerald and colleagues noted that it ignores or distorts substantive contrary data and is based on faulty logic.

The researchers referenced two empirical studies that suggested the lack of a scientific basis to the abuse defense. They were especially concerned that such unfounded claims may serve to undermine the integrity of meaningful scientific contributions to judicial decision making. They suggested this defense is part of a long and unfortunate history of denying the credibility of, and rationalizing the widespread existence of violence against, women.

Fitzgerald et al. (1999) lamented that like rape cases, claims of sexual harassment are all too frequently viewed with skepticism by opposing counsel, triers of fact, or other interested parties, despite the absence of credible data supporting that perspective. The researchers observed that, in addition to the frequent concern expressed by women's advocates regarding victims being put on trial, there is an insidious effort to distort real psychological science findings and expert testimony in order to prevail in a lawsuit. They concluded with an even more profound concern that victims are too frequently left behind and unheard, as opposing attorneys and opposing experts take attention-getting adversarial positions and vie for the court's attention. Experts can become the stars of these trials, often at the expense of real victims. However, more than 20 years later, evidence suggests that the vast majority of experts truly are just that, and they approach each case with rigorous scientific support.

Practical Guidance for Effective Expert Witness Testimony

Thornton et al. (2009) lamented that although I/O psychologists can add value in providing employment discrimination testimony, they may not adequately understand the judicial process, their roles as expert witnesses, or the court's perceptions of their testimony. They presented 10 pragmatic recommendations that are designed to enhance the effectiveness of expert witness testimony in employment discrimination litigation and that should be helpful to psychologists serving as expert witnesses in all types of litigation.

Some of the recommendations may be obvious, but an overview loosely adapted from their article and generously interspersed with my own experience may be helpful to psychologists serving as expert witnesses:

- If a case's professional merit is not immediately recognized by the expert, it is probably best to avoid accepting the case. Professional ethics as a psychologist require nothing less than the whole truth sworn under penalty of perjury (APA, 2017).

- Professional credentials are essential to getting to the point of admissibility, but the key to being effective is the ability to offer reliable testimony to the court (FRE 702, 2021).
- Experts stay current regarding professional literature. Any discrepancy noted by an opposing expert can and will be used to call the expert's credibility into question.
- About credibility—it is preferable for an expert to respond, "I do not know," in cross-examination rather than try to bluff through a response. Assume all parties are smart and know or at least sense when an expert is bluffing.
- Providing adequate explanatory detail for the court helps ensure the evidence provided meets the standards for relevance, as determined by the presiding judge upon objection by the opposing party (*Daubert v. Merrell Dow Pharmaceuticals, Inc.*, 1993). However, the expert should never volunteer information not required by the question, no matter which side asks the question. On the other hand, even if opposing counsel attempts to limit the expert to a "yes or no" response, the expert need not respond in kind, if there is no correct "yes or no" response. If my retaining attorney does not object, I turn to the judge and explain that I cannot fairly respond with a single word. Judges have ruled in my favor 100% of the time during those exchanges.
- If statistics are relevant and potentially helpful for a jury, it is appropriate to use them, but they need to be well explained. The court and the jury most likely do not have a good understanding of statistics and levels of significance. It is up to the expert to candidly and clearly explain any statistics that are part of testimony. This may be challenging, depending on the complexity of the statistics used. Keeping it simple and parsimonious is generally a good idea.
- Although experts are not permitted to testify about applicable laws, unless they are attorneys providing relevant expert testimony, it is important to have a good understanding of the various statutes and regulations that might relate to the testimony. This knowledge includes case law, especially precedent-setting decisions that relate to areas of expertise and testimony, as well as the FRE and the Federal Rules of

Civil Procedure and their state counterparts, if applicable. Experts are further cautioned to be aware of as many details/facts of the case as possible. This is a ripe area for opposing counsel to attempt to discredit the witness by demonstrating that the expert may have scientific knowledge, but the expert is deficient in being able to apply that knowledge to the facts of the case at hand.

- It is important to clarify the expert's role as an impartial witness—even though the expert has most likely been hired by one side in the litigation. The opposing side may try to position the testimony as biased based on whomever is paying for the time. This is a classic impeachment approach, in which the witness may be accused of being nothing more than a "hired gun." In my experience, juries are typically too sophisticated to readily succumb this tactic, unless the facts show there is some justification for them to do so. In order to avoid such labeling, it is helpful to have served as an expert for both plaintiffs and defendants over course of one's professional career.

- Understanding and being able to explain the practice of forensic consulting psychology is integral to the expert's testimony. Because the expertise required may not be obvious to the court, it is paramount to be able to explain the scientific basis for expert testimony—a common area for challenge to the testimony as being based on junk science.

JURORS' PERCEPTIONS OF EXPERT WITNESSES AND THEIR TESTIMONY

FCPs engaged in litigation support activities are often called upon to assess the level of methodological rigor utilized by testifying experts and to explain these issues and their probable impact on juror decision making. Chorn and Kovera (2019) evaluated how differences in the validity and reliability of psychological testing used by an expert influence evidence-credibility determination by judges, attorneys, and mock jurors. The researchers found that the level of methodological rigor did not make a difference in admissibility determinations by judges or in the decisions by attorneys to move to exclude evidence that was suspect. Perhaps most surprising to FCPs, cross-examination regarding methodological rigor, including issues of validity and reliability, did not assist jurors in assessing the efficacy of a testing protocol. Thus, Chorn and Kovera concluded that judges need to be educated to evaluate the quality and rigor of expert evidence. As stated in FRE 702 (a), the trier of fact needs to understand the expert testimony. Certainly, the expert's job is also to educate the trier of the law (i.e., the judge) when necessary, as well.

Expert Witness's Unique Status

DeMatteo et al. (2019) noted the unique privileged status that expert witnesses enjoy in the courtroom, as well as the power and influence they can wield. The authors also observed that the science underlying expert testimony is becoming more complex and perhaps more difficult for jurors to put in proper perspective when assessing expert testimony. The conclusion they drew is that judges must act in a "*Daubert*-mandated gatekeeping role" (p. 130). Simply stated, DeMatteo et al. are of the opinion that, because judges are in charge of the admissibility of expert testimony, those judges need to use more discretion in what evidence they admit.

McCarthy Wilcox and NicDaeid (2018) conducted research with actual jurors to understand the qualities of an expert that inspire confidence and contribute to their perceived credibility. Education and years of experience were found to be important. Jurors focused on academic qualifications, demeanor, and the level of confidence displayed by the expert in responding to questions and cross examination. This research is especially useful for FCPs engaged in witness vetting and preparation activities—the fidelity of the mock juror sample and the specificity of the results can inform identification and coaching of optimal witnesses.

There is an apparent consensus that when expert testimony is offered and a witness is accepted as an expert, the likelihood that a juror may give unwarranted deference to a witness's purported expertise, which may not be grounded in real science, becomes an issue. In his 2015 work, Prescott represented that such an expert designation by the court "is a powerful predictor of trial outcomes because the fact finder may give more weight to the credentials than actual reliability or validity of the scientific methodology" (p. 521). A challenge for jurors occurs when opposing expert testimony is in conflict, as often occurs during the course of litigation. Jurors must then make relative credibility determinations among the experts. This is a dilemma we address later in this chapter.

Townson (2016) conducted research to assess the perceptions jurors had about the knowledge and trustworthiness of expert witnesses. Prior to this time, the research reflected that expert witnesses were thought to be mercenary, police witnesses were seen to be untrustworthy, and eyewitnesses were unreliable. Townson utilized a rigorous experimental methodology, including video technology to enhance the fidelity of the simulation, and determined that the designation of a witness as an expert made jurors believe the witness to have greater knowledge and greater trustworthiness. Townson's research is significant because it was effectively controlled with only the label ascribed to witnesses added. The expert label alone appeared to have made the difference.

Wechsler et al. (2015) used an experimental and descriptive analysis to conclude that attorneys are more comfortable offering forensic science evidence through experts rather than psychological evidence in addition to expert testimony. Attorneys might have been concerned that the psychological evidence without context would be more difficult for jurors to understand and assimilate. The researchers concluded that attorneys were quite familiar with the dimensions that seem to influence the perception of expert credibility by jurors. They found that attorneys most highly valued expert knowledge, professional experience, communication ability, and trustworthiness—along with the content of an expert's work product.

An interesting but not surprising outcome of Wechsler et al.'s (2015) research was that attorneys were convinced that errors were more likely to occur in the work of experts engaged by other attorneys. However, Parrott et al. (2015) used a sample of mock jurors to discover otherwise. Parrott and colleagues found that high-knowledge experts did not enjoy greater credibility with mock jurors, nor did they gain greater agreement. Instead, high-knowledge experts were perceived as significantly less likeable than low-knowledge experts, for no logical reason, but perceived expertise and likeability did not influence mock jurors' decision making in any meaningful way. There were no significant gender differences. Readers might speculate that higher knowledge experts may have been more arrogant than their lower knowledge counterparts—and that was what the jury responded to—but the research did not assess that dimension.

Opposing Expert Testimony

With respect to attitudes regarding expert witness testimony, Levett and Kovera (2008) surprised many seasoned litigators with the results of their research demonstrating that the best way to educate jurors about damaging, but methodologically misleading, testimony by an opposing expert may not be the seemingly obvious choice to put up their own expert witness in rebuttal. Instead, they found that "the presence of opposing expert testimony caused jurors to be skeptical of all expert testimony rather than sensitizing them to flaws in the other expert's testimony" (p. 363). Indeed, jurors rendered more verdicts contrary to an opposing expert's testimony when that potentially damaging testimony was left entirely unrefuted by their own expert. Readers should be cautious about generalizing this finding, however, even though it was somewhat independent of the precise content of the opposing expert's testimony. The researchers concluded that, contrary to what they call the assumptions in the U.S. Supreme Court's *Daubert* decision, opposing expert testimony may not be the best safeguard against the introduction of "junk science" at trial.

Jones and Kovera (2015) engaged in research to determine whether visual aids, typically referred to as demonstrative evidence, could assist an opposing expert witness in sensitizing jurors to concerns about the veracity of evidence introduced by the other side and represented as scientifically valid. They found that jurors were able to adequately understand concerns about the lack of scientific rigor of a study prepared by a defense expert, when properly explained by an opposing expert, whether or not demonstrative evidence was utilized. But the researchers concluded that demonstrative evidence was still required for jurors to convert that understanding into an actual verdict determination. In litigation, it is the verdict that counts. This is consistent with my experience in trying to incorporate demonstrative evidence to support expert testimony, whenever appropriate (see Chapter 3, this volume).

Scobie et al. (2019) conducted research regarding the effectiveness of expert testimony in challenging the veracity of forensic evidence that had been introduced but not validated. Scobie et al. concluded that opposing expert testimony can influence the verdict, but the finding was mediated by the jurors' understanding of the methodological integrity that was employed by the expert.

Lieberman and Sales (2007) provided the following historical context:

> In 1975 Schulman founded the first professional trial consulting firm, the National Jury Project. . . . The following year, Donald Vinson, a marketing professor from the University of Southern California, was contacted by the law firm of Cravath, Swaine, and Moore to help in a large antitrust case brought against their client, IBM. . . . Vinson's success in the case led him to leave his position at the University of Southern California and create a company known as Litigation Sciences in 1979 (D. E. Vinson, personal communication, September 2, 2005). Over the next decade, Litigation Services became one of the leading firms providing selection services. Vinson sold the firm in 1987 and several years later created Decision Quest (http://www.decisionquest.com). This firm provided . . . consultation services for . . . the O. J. Simpson criminal trial. (p. 6)

After the Simpson trial, science-based trial and jury consultants played a significant role in high profile trials (e.g., Michael Jackson, Scott Peterson, Kobe Bryant, Martha Stewart). Because of the effectiveness of these services, a number of firms, in addition to sole practitioner FCPs, began forming to take advantage of the emerging proliferation of jury consulting firms. The trial and jury consultants utilized in these matters conducted the research in the respective trial venues and were effective in both predicting trial outcomes as well as assisting in the crafting of proposed juror questionnaires that revealed potential predispositions and biases.

D'Esposito (2016) noted that a courtroom is not a sanitized environment, and jurors pay attention to everything that is going on, regardless of any direction that they may receive from a judge. D'Esposito took a strong adversarial position against the trial consulting industry, maintaining that regulation is needed because the practice poses an unregulated danger to the objectivity of the courtroom. The concern is directed against the reliance on psychology and nonverbal communication to presumably manipulate a desired outcome.

Many FCPs are involved in HRM policy and practice, either as practitioners, consultants, or expert witnesses. To the extent that HRM can be viewed on a continuum from what has been referred to as a soft science to a rigorous, methodologically based science, forensic FCPs are likely to participate mostly within the hard science portion. Psychometrics and selection testing, as typically used in assessment centers, require the specialized training and skills of forensic professionals. It is the relationship of selection testing to job performance and productivity that commands the attention of forensic professionals.

There are challenges, however, when using psychometric instruments to screen out potentially low-performing workers in the service of increasing productivity by employees. Such presumably well-intentioned applications of the science of selection and assessment may also serve to differentially preclude opportunities and employment for otherwise qualified protected class members. Four decades ago, S. D. Norton and Gustafson (1982) argued that "a primary short-term goal of I/O psychology must be to change The Uniform Guidelines on Employee Selection Procedures, which are inconsistent with current research knowledge and professional practice" (p. 904). The authors predicted that as psychologists increase the use of cognitive ability tests for selection and promotion in organizations, the need for quotas or differential test cutoffs to reduce or mitigate the differences in scoring may not be related to actual differences in job performance. That prediction turned out to be quite accurate and is the essence of proper test validation, as well as the reduction of adverse impact not demonstrably related to actual job performance that may be triggered.

FCPs are often called upon to explain this and related test validity issues to juries in employment discrimination litigation. The difference between positive discrimination, which selection and promotion testing is designed to achieve, and unlawful discrimination may be a subtle and perhaps counterintuitive principle for triers of fact to apply without unbiased expert assistance. Whenever I have been asked to or have been allowed to use a flip chart to explain something to the jury, their attention is focused, and my response appears to be most effective. Trials can be long and dull for jurors, and anything that breaks through the tedium is a positive for their consideration—and for the expert. During one trial, I hand-calculated a chi square on a flip chart to test significance for an adverse impact analysis after opposing counsel claimed during cross-examination that I had simply fabricated the results to which I testified. The jury seemed fascinated and took many notes. The trial resulted in a multimillion-dollar verdict, and the attorneys later advised me that the jury thought my demonstration was significant for their understanding of the theory of the case and was a major contribution to their verdict.

Various federal laws protect seven to 10 specific "classes" from employment discrimination. The laws usually cited are the Civil Rights Act of 1964, the Age Discrimination in Employment Act (1967), and the Americans With Disabilities Act (ADA; 1990). The list of protected class characteristics varies according to the terminology of the list, and new ones are added as court decisions are published. In 2020, the list consisted of race, color, religion/creed, national origin/ancestry, sex, age, mental/physical disability, veteran status, genetic information, and citizenship. Of course, the laws are clear that given all circumstances, the applicant must be able to do the job being applied for with the employer making only "reasonable" accommodations (ADA, 1990). Farr and Tippins (2017) provided useful guidance for FCPs desiring additional information, in their authoritative *Handbook of Employee Selection*.

SUMMARY

This chapter defined and explored the unique role of the expert witness in litigation. The expert psychological witness may or may not be an FCP, but it should be noted that expert testimony consists of a two-part process: admissibility and weight. The history of admissibility dates back only to

1962 and the *Jenkins v. United States* case. Although the court in *Jenkins* determined that psychologist testimony was admissible, what the content of that testimony needed to be has had its own history from *Frye v. United States* in 1923, through the Federal Rules of Evidence, first enacted in 1975, to *Daubert v. Merrell Dow Pharmaceuticals, Inc.* in 1993. However, although the admissibility of expert testimony seems to have been determined both in state and federal courts, the weight the trier of fact should give to such testimony remains vague. The expert retains a unique status in the courts, and controversy remains regarding the deference and weight to be afforded their opinions by jurors and courts.

3

Understanding Jury Trials, Decision Making, and the Litigation Process

Jury trials have been humorously characterized by supporters as the worst possible system for dispensing justice—except for any other system in the world. Although in matters of criminal law, jury trials are guaranteed by the U.S. Constitution, bench trials are also an option at the request of the defendant (U.S. Const. amend. VI; U.S. Const. art. III, § 2). Used more extensively throughout the world, bench trials are hearings or trials in which the verdict is determined only by a judge or a panel of judges. In such cases, the judge serves as the trier of the law as well as the trier of fact. Note that many of the strategies and tactics utilized by litigation consultants in conjunction with jury trials, with some modifications, are also applicable to bench trials. Judges can be "researched" in much the same way that a prospective juror pool can be, although they are unlikely to be willing to fill out questionnaires or respond to voir dire questions,

https://doi.org/10.1037/0000295-003
Forensic Organizational Consulting: The Role of Psychologists in Litigation Support, by J. M. Finkelman with L. Gomberg

or to recuse themselves or be removed without a valid legal reason (i.e., a conflict of interest, personal involvement, or other identifiable problems).

More specifically, although the Sixth Amendment to the U.S. Constitution only guarantees a jury trial for criminal defendants, at the defendant's option, practically speaking for every legal matter (civil or criminal), the defendant is entitled to a trial by jury (see U.S. Const. art. III and Chapter 5 of this volume). However, in the United States, certain matters are considered cases in equity. The judge, and the judge alone, balances the equities in certain cases. Among those cases are most family proceedings and probate matters. These are matters that don't usually provide a monetary remedy.

One example of equity that comes to mind is Solomon (of the Old Testament) telling the arguing mothers who both claim to be the mother of a baby to cut the baby in half. The equitable remedy that Solomon found in that case was to give the baby to the woman who would have rather lost the baby than have her child be cut in half.

An equitable remedy is usually called *specific performance*, which makes the parties whole if at all possible. Different rules and defenses apply than to cases at law. For example, defendants in civil cases at law have the protection of Statutes of Limitations; in some states, breach of contract cases have 4-year time limitations to bring an action, and in some states personal injury cases have 2-year time limitations. In equity, the defense is "laches," or the need for plaintiffs to act in what the court determines is a timely manner to plead their cases (Garner, 2019). Equity is rife with maxims: Equity aids the vigilant, not those who slumber on their rights; he who comes into equity must come with clean hands, alternately referred to as the "clean hands doctrine" or "dirty hands doctrine"; both are favorites (Garner, 2019).

JUROR PERCEPTION AND DECISION MAKING

This chapter promises insight into jury trials, and the forensic consulting psychologist (FCP) is the logical person to provide that insight. After a particularly contentious trial, one in a series involving what used to be commonly referred to as a "Big 8 accounting firm," the defense attorneys wanted to gain insight about an unanticipated outcome, given that similar cases were about to be filed. After the jurors rendered their verdict in the trial and were leaving the courthouse, the attorneys asked who would be willing to be interviewed about the trial that just ended. This is a not uncommon and perfectly legal tactic, and it was fortunate that the foreperson volunteered. Because of my experience and reputation in the area, I was hired to interview him to determine what had just happened at trial.

The attorneys arranged for me to take the foreperson to lunch, with the understanding that I would be soliciting information about the deliberations that just resulted in the verdict. He was pleased to be invited and readily shared his experience and insights. After lunch, to my surprise, I was invited to his apartment to continue the conversation, noting that he still had more information to share. After several hours, I learned that the verdict had been largely based on a particular piece of demonstrative evidence introduced by the plaintiff's attorneys. The defense had not anticipated the evidence would be that pivotal and devastating for their theory of the case. The foreperson also provided insight as to which jurors were swayed the most by that evidence.

The information gleaned was deemed extremely valuable for the attorneys as they prepared the next defense for that client. They tested different ways to neutralize the damaging evidence using focus groups. They also gained understanding about the types of jurors most predisposed against their client, independent of the facts and evidence presented at trial. Interviewing jurors is a tried-and-true approach that attorneys and consulting psychologists continue to frequently use to get the most direct information about jury thinking and decision making.

The Law

Interestingly, there is a general rule that jury deliberations are confidential. Of course, the origin of this rule is based on protecting the jurors' right to speak honestly and freely during deliberations without fear of personal, professional, or legal repercussions (Federal Rules of Evidence [FRE] 606b, 2021). However, there is no rule that prevents a juror from volunteering information. The FRE case on point is *Warger v. Shauers* (2014), wherein a unanimous U.S. Supreme Court decision confirmed that FRE 606(b) even protects a juror's admission during deliberations that they lied during voir dire, even as that lie might have affected the ensuing verdict. The juror admitted during deliberations to having lied when asked if they knew anything about the specifics of the case to be presented. However, in *Pena-Rodriguez v. Colorado* (2017), the U.S. Supreme Court held, in a 5-to-3 decision, if the deliberations include racist/prejudicial statements, at least those parts of the deliberations are no longer protected or confidential.[1]

Media Exposure in Jury Perception and Decision Making

Understanding the complex dynamics of jury trials is understanding the intricacies of group decision making. FCPs are called upon to do this quite frequently in a consulting capacity. It is well understood in social psychology and group dynamics that the decision-making process shifts radically when individuals become part of groups, formal (as in juries) or informal (as in social clubs or among friends). There may be a question as to whether the legal system is best served by these group dynamics, and that issue is explored in this volume.

Judges are typically concerned about protecting jurors from any influences outside of their instructions or actual courtroom testimony and exhibits. Media reporting and trial publicity are particularly troublesome when known to jurors. Barthe et al. (2013) compared the television habits of Introduction to Criminal Justice students at two different universities and found that the students' beliefs and knowledge about the justice system, as well as selection of a major course of study, were influenced more by their media exposure than by their education and experience.

Barthe et al. (2013) concluded that "self-reported media exposure affected both perceptions of the justice system and major selection. Specifically, viewing law enforcement related television influenced major

---

[1] Just as an aside for "watchers" of the U.S. Supreme Court, the reason only eight justices participated in the 2017 decision is that Justice Scalia had died in 2016, and a replacement was not appointed until after the 2016 presidential election. The Senate refused to confirm then President Obama's nominee; instead, it confirmed Justice Neil Gorsuch after President Trump assumed office and nominated him in 2017.

selection, while forensic and court related shows negatively impacted perceptual accuracy" (p. 13). The fear is that mass media may be more influential within the justice system at the expense of fairness, accuracy, and objectivity in jury decision making than can accurately be measured.

Robbennolt and Studebaker (2003) provided additional research-based insight into how potent news media reporting can be in civil justice decision making, going beyond juror decision making. They concluded that the media have the potential to influence the entire civil litigation system in addition to the various participants in the process, including jurors and judges. The concern is their finding that news media present a consistently distorted picture of civil litigation that influences key perceptions and outcomes. Through targeted research, consulting psychologists can play an important role in helping to identify biased perceptions and improper influences—alerting the court to these factors so as to permit attorneys and judges to take corrective action as appropriate.

Emotions and Jury Decision Making

People are emotional beings, and that is understood and accepted. But as a society we often fail to consider the role of emotions in the way juries render a verdict in a legal contest. Baumann and Friehe (2012) determined that the outcome of litigation is changed when the role of emotions is considered and incorporated into the decision-making equation. "We show that emotions may increase or decrease individual and total equilibrium contest effort, introduce an asymmetry into the contest, and reinforce or weaken a plaintiff's incentives to bring a suit" (Baumann & Friehe, 2012, p. 195). The concern is whether the introduction of emotions degrades the decision-making process and thus potentially the accuracy of verdicts that are rendered. It is troublesome, although not surprising, that emotions, rather than objective logic, may serve to influence the propensity of plaintiffs to initiate a lawsuit. This also may inform the prevalence of frivolous litigation (discussed in Chapter 1, this volume).

There are few areas in which psychology and the legal system interact more dramatically and perhaps unpredictably. Unfortunately, emotions are also a domain over which the courts have little control. Although it is true that emotions can be measured and categorized to some extent, that is not sufficient to permit their influence to be neutralized. Despite that limitation, consulting psychologists can utilize other tools to detect bias and anticipate outcomes—which can be useful for litigators on both sides to understand as they develop case strategies.

Psychological Theory and Jury Decision Making

As has been and will be demonstrated throughout this volume, psychology is intricately tied to the law in many areas but none more directly than with respect to jury decision making. Although it might be difficult to generate an exact percentage, it seems reasonable to surmise that a significant portion of the variance associated with juries rendering consistent verdicts (or to use the more psychological term, the lack of interrater reliability among juries) can be accounted for by understanding the underlying psychological factors. In many ways, that is what FCPs and jury consultants attempt to do. The accuracy of prediction is a function of the scientific rigor used in the analysis and, of course, the integrity of the available data.

Bornstein and Greene (2011) argued that the way juries perceive and recall trial evidence, coupled with the dynamics of the group decision-making process, can best be characterized as basic cognitive and social psychology principles. The authors noted that juries provide a real-world laboratory for examining theoretical issues related to reasoning, memory, judgment and decision making, attribution, stereotyping, persuasion, and group behavior. Conversely, psychological research can inform trial procedures, enabling juries to benefit from fairer procedures and reach better outcomes (Bornstein & Greene, 2011, p. 63). Their conclusion was that the jury decision-making process can inform psychological theory that in turn can drive legal policy making.

The law follows psychology. Although no definitive source can be found to attribute the origin of this statement, the statement is a truism. Examples can be found in family law, most recently when the U.S. Supreme Court recognized that marriage is a fundamental human right and obviated the man and woman marriage distinction as pertaining to U.S. law (*Obergefell v. Hodges*, 2015). Twelve years earlier, with a juvenile law case, the U.S. Supreme Court had recognized what psychologists had been teaching for years: The human brain is not fully developed until adulthood, and juveniles should not be treated the same as adults in certain criminal matters, especially when it comes to sentencing (*Roper v. Simmons*, 2005). Further examples can be found in criminal law as far back as 1843, in England, when the court recognized that if a party couldn't form the intent to commit a specific crime, the law couldn't punish the action (*Queen v. M'Naghten*, 1843)—and even in probate and tax law where the U.S. Supreme Court invalidated the Defense of Marriage Act, which had disallowed same-sex, validly married spouses' estate tax exemptions (*United States v. Windsor*, 2013).

Juror Attitude and Decision Making

Lecci and Myers (2008) determined that the Pretrial Juror Attitude Questionnaire (PJAQ) demonstrates superior predictive validity over more traditional measures of pretrial bias. The importance for research-driven decision making by consulting psychologists is that it supports the utility and justifies the cost of utilizing empirical scientific methodologies to assist attorneys in avoiding detrimental bias in selection of jurors—the triers of fact. The constructs that proved effective were theoretically derived, as assessed by other scales, as well as some that were new to the research literature. The attitudes assessed by the PJAQ are conviction proneness, system confidence, cynicism toward the defense, racial bias, social justice, and innate criminality. Although some litigators remain confident in relying on their gut instincts as to which prospective jurors to select or avoid, empirically based decision making remains the preferred option for reducing the probability of juror bias.

Lieberman et al. (2016) sought to categorize the range of methodological rigor associated with jury decision-making research practice by surveying the perception of professionals involved in conducting, reviewing, and publishing jury research. The researchers noted considerable variability over time in the methodology used to conduct experimental jury decision-making research. Multiple variables have been manipulated and reviewed for this type of research, and the acceptability of different research approaches ultimately becomes a subjective judgment call. The inclusion of jury instructions was considered to be the most important trial element for research purposes, whereas deliberation was least important. The authors advocated for more focused research on the creation and delivery of more objective jury instructions, which seems necessary and appropriate.

Nuñez et al. (2011) raised a legitimate methodological concern with respect to research regarding jury decision making. They noted that jury research concerns have focused predominantly on sample subject selection and the propriety of using students versus nonstudents as mock jurors. The subject sample issue is discussed later in this chapter. Although sample selection is a legitimate area for challenging certain jury research studies, it may not be the most salient and predictive issue. Rather, the authors argued that researchers are ignoring the more relevant variable of jury deliberation. They contended that the lack of information regarding juror deliberations in research "is a much greater threat to ecological validity and that some of our basic findings and conclusions in the literature today might be different if we had used juries, not non-deliberating jurors" (Nuñez et al., 2011, p. 439). From a group dynamics perspective, their position makes considerable sense. Psychologists understand how group interaction can change perspectives and opinions—and that is what actually takes place during a jury trial, even though jury deliberations are, by law, confidential.

Tabak et al. (2014) utilized simulated jury decision making through online focus groups to evaluate the applicability of computer-mediated communications to a mock jury deliberation study, in lieu of surveying individual jurors in order to analyze and understand the decision-making process that is used in reaching a verdict. Logically, they were able to demonstrate that knowledge of how juries deliberate could improve our understanding of how verdicts are reached. They concluded that electronic mock juries could be a useful addition to traditional jury deliberation research because of their time and cost efficiencies, as well as providing wider recruitment opportunities. This is an important option for consulting psychologists to consider, due to the increasing cost sensitivity of their attorney clients, as well as the time pressure to provide results once they are retained to assist in a matter that is going to trial.

Effects of Voir Dire on Juror Bias and Decision Making

Hamilton and Zephyrhawke (2015) raised intriguing issues that should be familiar to consulting psychologists versed in bias and decision-making research. The language of a question can be very influential as to the type of response it elicits. This phenomenon is particularly relevant in change of venue surveys that litigation consultants are often asked to facilitate. The objective is to determine the degree of antidefendant bias in each venue from which the jury pool might be selected. Given the importance of preexisting attitudes in determining a jury verdict at trial, this is more than a theoretical issue.

Hamilton and Zephyrhawke (2015) discovered that traditionally worded voir dire questions severely underestimated the degree of anti-defendant bias in their study. About 4% of their sample responded that they doubted their ability to assume innocence, when in questioning actual jurors, it was one out of every three or four people sampled—a dramatic distortion that could have significant consequences at trial. Words matter.

Juror Perception of Trial Consultants

Griffith et al. (2007) surveyed 1,251 potential jurors in all 50 states and found that participants who believed the legal system was fair, participants with higher incomes, and Anglo Americans viewed trial consultants most positively. Interaction effects and variance overlap among these predictors are likely. The survey also revealed an expectation that trial consultants were used in 43% of all trials. Of those responding, 18% admitted that they would be more likely to favor the side not using trial consultants—if they had that information. The researchers cautioned trial consultants to consider the potential impact of their presence at trial.

In my experience, trial consultants who need to be present at trial, rather than those doing focus group research ahead of trial, prefer to remain as anonymous and unobtrusive as possible in the visitors' gallery of the courtroom. One rarely sees them conferring with counsel, although they may be sending text messages during jury selection, unless prohibited by a particular court for all visitors. There seems to be a tacit understanding that this type of assistance might prejudice the judge and/or the jury against their side in the case. Unlike expert witnesses who are expected to offer neutral and balanced testimony, regardless of whether that occurs, trial consultants are expected to be partisan. Much like the attorneys, they are unambiguously advocating for the party who hired them.

Robertson et al. (2012) extended research regarding the perception of jury consultants to also consider the perception of the credibility and trial testimony of expert witnesses (see Chapter 2, this volume). They explored whether "blinded experts" would be more persuasive to a jury than more traditional experts, hired by one side or the other. In a blind review of the evidence at trial, a neutral intermediary selects and pays a professionally qualified expert who does not know which side might be seeking expert opinions or testimony. This approach is similar to the rationale that lies behind the use of outside blind reviews that peer-reviewed journals typically employ to ensure an unbiased assessment of research and writing with the goal to provide journalistic and scientific integrity.

Not surprisingly, the researchers found that blind experts, testifying for either side, were perceived as significantly more credible and demonstrably more persuasive than experts specifically hired directly by one side. This outcome occurred despite an understanding that all expert witnesses are sworn and obligated to provide neutral (truthful) testimony, regardless of which side hires and pays them. Practically speaking, if an expert's testimony isn't going to help the side that hires them, the expert will be paid, thanked, and dismissed from employment prior to that testimony ever being introduced as evidence. Judges often try to facilitate proper consideration of expert testimony through special jury instructions (see Chapters 4 and 5).

Juror Perception of Physical Attractiveness and Unattractiveness

Manthorpe (2019) observed that, although the public has always appreciated and elevated the status of individuals deemed as attractive, the extension of that adulation to courtroom settings has the compromising capacity to alter verdict determinations and thus undermine the fair and equal treatment of all litigants by juries. The author noted that unattractive people do not do as well as attractive people in litigation. Research seems to back up this assertion: In 2017, Hollier conducted a meta-analysis of 27 studies and was surprised to find the extent to which this seemed to be the reality of litigation. Unattractive criminal defendants get longer sentences, assailants of unattractive victims get shorter sentences, and unattractive plaintiffs get less compensation. This is obviously not how the legal system was intended to operate.

"JUNK SCIENCE" REVISITED

It has become apparent that litigants, both plaintiffs and defendants, perceive the utility of characterizing as much of the support for their position as possible based on a scientific foundation. It is also apparent that opposing attorneys typically feel compelled to challenge the scientific foundation of the opposing case, often characterizing it as based on "junk science" (Giannelli, 1993; see also Chapter 1, this volume). The intent is to persuade the court to preclude its admissibility or establish the basis for an appeal if they are not successful. The thinking is that the most effective way to refute the anticipated damaging testimony of an opposing expert is to block that witness from testifying. Hence the so-called junk science defense has unfortunately become increasingly prevalent among many types of civil and criminal forms of litigation described in this volume.

Although the FRE, the *Daubert* case, and state codes and cases provide general rules, admissibility standards vary by jurisdiction. This variance can be especially contentious when a novel scientific theory or methodology is advanced by an opposing expert. A case can be made for the position that there is a developing science and art for refuting the admissibility of damaging purportedly scientific testimony from the other side. The courts have already affirmed certain precedent-setting evidence standards, such as with the ubiquitous *Daubert* Standard used in federal courts. Remembering that *Daubert v. Merrell Dow Pharmaceuticals, Inc.* was decided in 1993, and it does not mandate the states to follow, various state jurisdictions continue to use the 1923 *Frye* test, some variation of it, or a hybrid of *Frye* and *Daubert* to determine admissibility of expert testimony. Adding to the mix is the judge's discretion as to admissibility regarding the interpretation of the FRE, and it becomes clear why attorneys routinely invoke a variety of these arguments against the admissibility of testimony by opposing experts (USLegal.com, n.d.; see also Chapter 2, this volume). However, Cohen (1997) noted that some judges are more likely to rely on the adversarial process of cross-examination to test the veracity or speciousness of challenged scientific theories and methodologies. The underlying concern for the litigants is whether jurors will succumb too quickly to the allure of scientific sounding arguments and misconstrue them as being synonymous with the truth.

Attorneys also need to keep in mind that admissibility of expert testimony is only the first part of the problem. Once the testimony is admitted, the other part of the problem is the weight the jury gives that testimony. No amount of jury instructions can or should tell a juror how important a particular piece of evidence or testimony is. Although touched on in the discussion of standards of proof in the first chapter, a legal maxim certainly bears repeating in any discussion of weight of the evidence: It is the quality of the evidence presented that should be taken into the jury room, not the quantity. Cohen (1997) advised testifying psychologists as follows:

> Psychologists drawn into or appearing by choice in civil and criminal litigation would be well advised to critically evaluate the bases or foundation for their opinions in light of the admissibility standards being applied in the jurisdiction. Where there is some question about whether the proposed testimony can meet the jurisdictional standard, psychologists should consider what additional support can be mustered and how the bases for the testimony can best be presented to persuade the trial judge to let the jury consider it in deciding the case. (p. 407)

This is sound advice that should caution and inform all consulting psychologists who might be asked to offer expert opinions and/or share professional practice and policy information with the jury.

Edwards and Mnookin (2016) lamented that courts are relying too heavily on forensic expert testimony rather than challenging the validity and scientific underpinnings of the techniques they employ. The law relies on consistency, predictability, and equal treatment. The problem is that it is common for judges to default to forensic techniques without demonstrated validity but with a long track record of being used at trial. Just using an invalid technique repeatedly and training other practitioners to do the same through apprenticeship programs does not serve to develop scientific integrity that courts can rely on.

Although some judges have restricted the language that forensic experts can use in describing the applicability of evidence, the concern is that this is insufficient to have an impact on the understanding of jurors as to the validity of the supposedly scientific evidence that is presented to them by experts. Edwards and Mnookin (2016) contended that the practice of a court relying on adversarial testimony by experts to uncover issues surrounding the validity and reliability of forensic evidence that is presented is not warranted. Thus, junk science continues to make its way into the courtroom, despite the efforts of judges to control the misuse and mischaracterization of evidence.

"Junk Science," *Daubert*, and Criminal Trials

Consulting psychologists may be more frequently engaged to consult or testify in civil trials, but the empirical approaches and techniques they are qualified to employ are equally applicable to criminal trials. Luongo (2018) addressed the various scandals that are undermining criminal defense work and the application of valid scientific principles to related litigation. Bad science, unqualified experts, minimal government oversight, dishonest research, and crime labs that are overwhelmed are all exacting a cost on the integrity of litigation consulting for criminal trials.

Luongo (2018) advocated for having the federal judiciary develop rules of evidence that would preclude scientific evidence being improperly admitted under a hearsay exception. *Hearsay* is a statement originally made out of court by a party who hasn't been sworn that is then brought into court and offered as fact (FRE 801, 2021). The basic reason that hearsay is not admissible is that, no matter how relevant, its prejudicial effect out-weighs its probative value, except in several unique circumstances (see Chapters 1, 3, and 5). In fact, there are dozens of exceptions to this general rule, and some of them have even been codified (see FRE 803, 2021). Forensic psychology is most vulnerable to distortion and misuse, in part because it carries the aura of science and therefore may sound compelling to jurors, despite lacking the efficacy of true science, when applied by unqualified practitioners. This makes junk science doubly dangerous because its misuse in court serves to undermine confidence in the application of true scientific methodology and defensible research in credible litigation support activities by qualified practitioners, including consulting psychologists.

Hilbert (2019) drew similar conclusions to those articulated by Luongo (2018) and lamented what is characterized as the disappointing history of science in the courtroom, especially with respect to the intrusion of junk science to criminal cases. The author noted that some pundits have warned the very viability of the court system may be in jeopardy, although that probably overstates the risk.

According to Hilbert (2019), the repeatedly discussed case of *Daubert v. Merrell Dow Pharmaceuticals, Inc.* (1993) provided some of the much-needed reform regarding the admissibility of unqualified expert testimony. Previously, trial courts were imposing inconsistent and sometimes indefensible standards to determine which experts would be permitted to testify before a jury and what might constitute junk science. But that concern may not have been adequately corrected through *Daubert*, according to Hilbert, who expressed skepticism as to whether it is accomplishing its objectives and living up to expectations.

Neal et al. (2019) conducted a comprehensive investigation of psychological assessments being used in court by forensic mental health professionals, considering both legal standards and psychometric theory. The researchers determined that an impressive 90% of the assessment tools introduced as evidence by psychologists were supported by actual empirical testing. Approximately two thirds of the instruments were considered generally accepted by the professional community, although only about 40% were positively reviewed in authoritative sources, such as the

Mental Measurements Yearbook. It may be concerning to consulting psychologists, focused on methodological rigor and experimental integrity, that only about 5% of assessment instruments and approaches were ever challenged as to their admissibility (mostly based on lack of validity)—and these few challenges were only effective in about a third of these instances in having these instruments excluded.

Neal et al. (2019) lamented that there were very few challenges to the most scientifically indefensible instruments and technologies. And attorneys were typically reluctant to challenge expert assessments, perhaps because they were not confidant of their skill sets to do so. Even when attorneys did initiate challenges, judges often did not take appropriate action to exclude the improper evidence. This is obviously concerning and can result in an upsurge of junk science intruding at trial.

Prescott (2015) asked whether forensic experts are dispensing true science or if their authority to offer their opinions to a jury is more a function of "Privilege-by-License" (p. 521). This is a complex issue that has broad ethical as well as legal ramifications. Expert opinions interact with the rules of inclusion and exclusion that are the essence of the legal process for admitting testimony. Experts deemed qualified by a court are granted the unique privilege of being permitted to offer an opinion grounded in facts that have not been introduced as evidence and information coming from other parties and outside sources not vetted by the court.

Some experts are licensed, such as certain types of psychologists, which may afford an additional level of protection relative to unlicensed practitioners or professions that are not governed by licensure law (e.g., physicists, biologists, chemists). This usually includes industrial and organizational psychologists and consulting psychologists as well, although some are also licensed as psychologists, but they are not required to be so licensed. Of course, a license is not a guarantee of scientifically based and objective expert opinions and testimony.

Prescott (2015) expressed concerns regarding courts routinely admitting testimony without adequate consideration of its scientific veracity, validity, reliability, or even relevance. Because incentives to provide testimony may, in part, be financial and litigants vary significantly in their socioeconomic status and diversity, the potential for abuse must be considered. Evidentiary rules of exclusion may not operate equitably given these disparities. The result, according to the author, is that, in certain circumstances, there may be less science than informed estimation. Disguising moral or business judgments as science can undermine the integrity of the legal system.

Popular Culture in the Practice of Law

It is increasingly apparent that cultural context must be considered in order to understand the actual practice of law. The popular perception of litigants, often determined or largely influenced by popular culture, is a compelling factor in a jury's determination of corporate misconduct. It probably shouldn't be, but it has become a reality with which litigation consultants must contend. And like most variables in psychology and life, it doesn't operate in isolation. In my experience, there is an interaction effect that occurs with an awareness of how powerful and influential an organization may be. This interaction can cut in two directions: Organizations that are favorably perceived become even more respected when they are thought to be powerful and thus able to effectively implement good things in the world. But organizations that are unfavorably perceived, or associated with evil, are thought to be more dangerous and malevolent when they are powerful. This results in the assumption that more powerful organizations are better able to do bad things in the world.

Admittedly, this sounds a bit simplistic, but it is exactly what happens. A lot of insight can be gained regarding disposition to favor or disfavor litigants, especially corporate defendants in civil litigation, by determining into which of four categories they are perceived to fall, as follows:

1. Powerful and Good (as corporate citizens): This is the ideal and most favorable organizational scenario—liked and thought to be capable of doing the most good for society.
2. Powerful and Evil: This is the least favorable organizational scenario—disliked and thought to be most dangerous for society.
3. Weak and Good: This is a positively regarded, but ineffectual, organizational scenario—liked but not respected by juries.

4. Weak and Evil: This is a negatively regarded but less concerning organizational scenario—disliked but thought to be impotent and thus relatively innocuous by juries.

The implication for jury decision making is that organizations perceived to be in the first category are most likely to be treated leniently by juries, regardless of their actual conduct, while organizations perceived to be in the second are most likely to be treated harshly, regardless of their actual conduct. Although this outcome may not have been empirically reviewed, the methodology has been effectively utilized by successful litigation consulting firms that I have witnessed, including those with which I have been associated.

INDIVIDUAL PROCESSING STYLE AND JUROR BIAS

Gunnell and Ceci (2010) used cognitive experiential self-theory to determine whether individuals influenced by the experiential system (known as *E-processors*) are more likely to be susceptible to improper and irrational biases unrelated to the facts of a legal case, such as defendant attractiveness, than those influenced by the rational system (known as *R-processors*). Research subjects reviewed a criminal trial transcript and the defendant's profile and determined what they perceived to be an appropriate verdict and sentence. The researchers found that while E-processors and R-processors convicted attractive defendants at similar rates, E-processors were more likely to convict the less attractive defendants and render more lenient sentences for the more attractive defendants. Gunnell and Ceci concluded that their results "support an 'unattractive harshness' effect during guilt determination, an attraction leniency effect during sentencing and increased susceptibility to extralegal factors within E-processors" (p. 850).

For many practicing FCPs with actual courtroom experience, this is not a surprise. That attractiveness matters fits the stereotype of the utility of attractiveness in so many aspects of life and employment. However, it is particularly troublesome in a legal environment in which crucial matters of guilt or innocence and sentencing are supposed to be based only on the actual evidence presented at trial, not on extraneous or irrelevant factors, such as the physical appearance of the defendant or, for that matter, the physical appearance of attorneys representing either side. Justice may not be served when this type of bias manifests itself, but as was stated earlier, emotional reactions cannot be controlled.

Bias

The possibility of juror bias based on race, gender, and/or ethnicity is a perennial concern for FCPs and, of course, for the courts. In ideal circumstances, demographic variables should not even have to be considered in selecting a jury. But, in reality, research confirms that depending on the focus of a trial, these variabilities may have a significant impact on a juror's decision-making process and thus on their ability to render a fair and unbiased verdict. This is more than a theoretical concern, and experienced trial lawyers and judges understand just how much variance these demographics can account for in a jury verdict.

Therefore, the preselection questioning of potential jurors or voir dire is necessary; the actual art, science, and methods of voir dire are considered in depth throughout this volume. Although techniques and approaches will differ, the intent is always to predict the likelihood of juror bias that could interfere with their ability to render a fair verdict based only on the evidence presented at trial, rather than on preconceived prejudicial stereotypes. It would be naïve to assume that both sides in a trial are equally motivated to remove all sources of bias. More likely, litigators prefer to remove jurors who might be predisposed against whichever side they represent—but not those jurors predisposed to favor their client.

In his 2019 article, Coughlan questioned why biased jurors are still being empaneled, even after questioning by the attorneys. The U.S. Supreme Court recognized the impropriety of attorneys seeking to eliminate prospective jurors without proof of actual prejudice. Coughlan recommended that courts make jury selection the responsibility of a presumably objective trial consultant, rather than the partisan attorneys. There is also a recommendation of a state licensing board for trial consultants, as well as training to guide them regarding the use of scientific methodology and research data, rather than stereotypes, to determine juror bias.

Consulting psychologists engaged in litigation support and specifically jury selection need to be familiar with the previously mentioned Pretrial Juror Attitude Questionnaire (PJAQ). Lundrigan et al. (2016) reminded consulting psychologists how important this measure can be in predicting jury verdicts. An interesting, but not unexpected, finding was that the relationship and predictivity of pretrial attitudes and ultimate jury verdicts was mediated by jurors' interpretation of what beyond reasonable doubt (BRD) means operationally. The researchers found that both the PJAQ and BRD were significant independent predictors of ultimate jury verdicts.

The Law

Through a very short series of cases, the judiciary has taken steps to limit overt juror bias in certain instances. Usually it is the defense (but it can be either side) that makes a motion that the other side has used (usually) peremptory challenges to disqualify jurors based on a recognizable group, such as race, gender, and even sexual preference. Although jurors can be dismissed by either side through the use of challenges (either peremptory or for cause), because peremptory challenges are limited in number and no reason for dismissal need be given, the true motive of the challenge may not be readily noticeable until a pattern is established. This issue has been addressed in two cases almost a decade apart, which arose from two different jurisdictions (California and the federal courts). These cases have been combined when a party makes a Batson-Wheeler motion (*Batson v. Kentucky*, 1986; *People v. Wheeler*, 1978). In both cases, the prosecution systematically excluded Black jurors when a Black defendant was being tried. Investigation into motivation overwhelmingly showed that the striking of the Black individuals was based only on race. The final decisions in the appeals of both cases resulted in courts universally recognizing the propriety of the Batson-Wheeler challenge.

The Process

What is now referred to as the *Batson framework* requires a three-step process comprised of the responsibility of the trial judge to be certain the motion is made outside the hearing of the jury (this is made in a sidebar), the responsibility to pay close attention to jury selection, and the responsibility to be sure to give each side full and fair time to thoroughly question all potential jurors (*Bench Memorandum Re: Batson-Wheeler*, n.d.). Finally, the decision as to who made the best case will rest with the judge. If the exclusion is found not to have been race neutral, the result can be sanctioning the attorney, or even a mistrial can be declared with a new trial required, depending on the point in the proceedings in which the motion is made and granted.

Peremptory Challenges in General

Hunt (2015) reviewed the extensive research regarding the influence of race, ethnicity, and culture on the judgment and behavior of juries. One conclusion was that jurors were tougher on defendants from different racial and ethnic groups than their own. The research also demonstrated that jurors were more likely to vote in favor of death sentences for Black and Latino defendants convicted of crimes against White victims. "However, these effects are moderated by several factors related to the trial parties, context, and crime. Further, juror bias often involves subtle or implicit psychological processes that can be difficult to recognize and correct" (Hunt, 2015, p. 269).

Peremptory challenges continue to be controversial and divisive, despite their long history in trial courts. The difference of opinion is whether these challenges facilitate fair and impartial juror selection and trials or whether the strikes are used for discriminatory purposes. The U.S. Supreme Court's *Batson v. Kentucky* (1986) test was designed to determine whether the strikes were being used appropriately or with deliberate racial discrimination intent. The concern was and is that Black jurors are systematically being kept off juries by prosecutors and that they are not selected for service in proportion to their numbers in potential jury pools.

Daly (2015) suggested that peremptory challenges are often misused, and the *Batson v. Kentucky* decision does not provide the protection that the U.S. Supreme Court intended. The implication is that the effort of many prosecutors to offer a race-neutral rationale for striking Black jurors is often bogus and should not automatically be accepted by the courts. In *Foster v. Chatman* (2016), the Court ruled that prosecutors had deliberately removed every qualified Black potential juror and had done so with apparent discriminatory intent. Deference should not be granted to questionable race-neutral justifications for peremptory strikes of Black jurors.

COST-EFFECTIVE JURY CONSULTING

The business world has become increasingly more cost conscious, and it was inevitable that consciousness would migrate to litigation consulting as well. Although many types of trial consulting will be described in this volume, they are not equally cost-effective. Lambert (1994) observed (and anticipated) this trend of controlling costs more than 25 years ago, and it has become the new reality with respect to most jury consulting. In fact, I participated in elaborate high-stakes trial consulting with aggregate costs in excess of $1 million. But the stakes were many multiples of the costs, and the incremental utility of small additions to predictive power was quite significant.

To Hire or Not to Hire

As far back as 1994, Lambert explained,

> Lawyers for companies know that a "shadow jury" sits through the trial and reports daily on its impressions so that lawyers can get a sense of what the real jury may be thinking. But they also know that "shadow juries" often aren't worth the expense. (p. B7)

That may or may not still be an accurate assessment, depending on circumstances and what is at stake at trial. The challenge is that the ultimate level of risk is typically uncertain until the jury renders a verdict. A litigator's faulty instinct can be very costly for a client. This is a classic risk/benefit analysis. If an attorney can achieve a positive outcome at lesser cost, that person is a hero. But if the result of frugality proves to be a loss at trial, the savings was short sighted and obviously misguided. The loss is all that will be remembered and what litigators and their clients dread most. In many ways, litigation research is a form of trial insurance that may or may not be necessary or have utility in a given circumstance. Even after the verdict is rendered, the utility of the extra costs may not be known. Of course, if as in the earlier example, one side or the other is fortunate enough to be able to interview a juror, the benefit of the extra cost may become apparent. But questions remain:

- Would the same outcome have occurred without spending all that money?
- Exactly where was the turning point that triggered the verdict?

Campo (2015) cautioned that all similarly seeming trials are not alike, and he cautioned against consultants and attorneys trying to save money by skipping actual research in such cases. Although it may be tempting to rely on a consultant's prior experience in making assessments about trial strategy and probable outcomes, it is a risky path with high error probability, which can be very costly in the long run and create a false economy. The alternative is well known to consulting psychologists in the form of professionally conducted focus groups, which Campo referred to as feedback groups.

Readers are cautioned to not assume that feedback groups or focus groups will be predictive or empirically evaluative, because they are not intended as such and are not empirical research. Rather, if properly conducted, they can provide helpful qualitative feedback from a group similar to the likely juror pool in a specific venue. This is an important distinction that litigation consultants may need to stress with their attorney-clients, who may be inclined to treat this type of feedback as though it is empirically determined and thus demonstrably valid.

Juror Research Sample Derivation

One of the most cost-effective ways to conduct jury research is with the most commonly utilized research sample: undergraduate college students. The issue that frequently emerges is whether such samples are representative of juror pools. Bornstein et al. (2017) reviewed 53 studies and conducted a sophisticated meta-analysis to determine the efficacy and generalizability of jury simulation research utilizing student mock jurors. Their main finding was that guilty verdicts, culpability, and damage awards did not change significantly, regardless of the research sample that was engaged. "Furthermore, the variables that revealed significant or marginally significant differences, sentencing and liability judgments, had small or contradictory effect sizes (e.g., effects on dichotomous and continuous liability judgments were in opposite directions)" (Bornstein et al., 2017, p. 13). Thus, concerns about utilizing student samples in jury research may not always be justified, at least with respect to these outcome variables. Consulting psychologists will understand that there are always case-specific factors that must be considered in jury research, independent of the derivation of the sample.

The Law's Impact on Cost-Effectiveness

As was mentioned in the opening vignette in Chapter 1, in all civil litigation the potential monetary award must be considered. The most common types of damages in civil lawsuits are compensatory, general and special, and punitive. Compensatory damages are just that: They compensate the plaintiff for the loss suffered. According to the law, wrongful acts have a monetary value, so general damages are those that are generally awarded for the particular type of injury (i.e., some jurisdictions limit "pain and suffering" tort recovery to specified amounts), and special damages are those suffered by this particular plaintiff (i.e., lost wages). Punitive damages are awarded to punish the defendant for the intentional or grossly negligent act that caused the plaintiff's suffering and are based merely on what the trier of fact, usually the jury, sees as the egregiousness of the wrong. Breach of contract suits do not result in an award of punitive damages, unless there is a finding that the breach was the result of some tortious behavior (Legal Information Institute, Breach of Contract, n.d.). Again, the risks of an adverse judgment must be balanced with the cost of the litigation—for the plaintiff as well as the defendant.

SPECIFIC CIVIL LITIGATION: EMPLOYMENT DISCRIMINATION

Nielsen et al. (2010) studied 15 years of employment discrimination lawsuits filed in federal court and found that category of litigation "consists overwhelmingly of individual cases, a majority of which end in a small settlement. The outcomes of cases are difficult to predict at the outset of litigation" (p. 175). Their insight is useful in explaining the perception that the economics of utilizing consulting psychologists in a litigation support capacity may not be cost-effective. But without understanding the context, it can be a very misleading conclusion.

In my experience and through my own research, I have found that most employment discrimination cases filed in both state and federal courts result in small settlements or defense verdicts. Without knowing whether litigation support was utilized in each case, it is logically impossible to determine whether the outcome might have been significantly different absent litigation support by consulting psychologists or other professionals.

There is a need to differentiate cases based on the egregiousness of the alleged improper conduct to better assess the prophylactic role of consulting psychologists for the defense. Some small employment cases may be considered nuisance or even frivolous. When averaged with all such cases, they may serve to dilute the average size of employment discrimination lawsuit settlements. This is the classic fallacy of overinterpreting arithmetic means.

The United States Supreme Court

Serendipitously, as this chapter was being written, the U.S. Supreme Court published its 6–3 decision in *Bostock v. Clayton County* (2020). *Bostock* definitively stated that any employer who terminated an employee based mainly or substantially on that employee's sexual or gender preference was in violation of Title VII of the Civil Rights Act of 1964. The Court consolidated three cases from three different federal appellate jurisdictions (the Eleventh, Sixth, and Second Circuits) from Southern, Midwestern, and Eastern states (Georgia, Michigan, and New York) where the facts were similar: Employees had been fired when the employer found out the employee was gay or transgender. Justice Neil Gorsuch (surprisingly to some) wrote for the majority:

> An employer who fires an individual for being homosexual or transgender fires that person for traits or actions it would not have questioned in members of a different sex. Sex plays a necessary and undisguisable role in the decision, exactly what Title VII forbids. (*Bostock v. Clayton County*, 2020, ¶1)

The three justices who dissented seemed to have done so because they thought the wording of Title VII prohibiting sex discrimination in employment applied only to gender discrimination in employment and that the majority were making judicial law rather than leaving lawmaking up to Congress. The majority's response was that if Congress had thought about sexual preference and gender identity in 1964, these issues would have certainly been included.

Anderson (2020) appears to have taken a position that sided with the dissent that is skeptical of the Supreme Court majority decision, noting that attorneys for plaintiffs were asking the Court to recraft civil rights laws, such that they directly weaken one of the main objectives to protect the rights of women and girls. Anderson maintained that Congress did not legislate this outcome, and the U.S. Supreme Court is cautioned not to appropriate Congress's domain and authority by adopting such extreme positions. Anderson argued that it is Congress, rather than the Court, that can craft policy to include sexual orientation and gender identity that are actually quite distinct from biological sex. Consulting psychologists should recognize the serious employment implications of this contrary position that is still held by many in organizational settings and society.

Application of Jury Consulting to Civil and Criminal Trials

Morgan and Palk (2013) observed that although forensic psychology is typically associated with the criminal and family law domains, it is ideally suited to offer skills and knowledge in the civil law domain. The authors maintained that civil law is the least represented legislative domain with respect to psychological research and professional commentary. They reminded all forensic psychologists that their practice inevitably takes place within legal environments. There is no question but that the skill sets of consulting psychologists, as highlighted throughout this volume, are equally applicable to civil, criminal, and family law matters. For example, competency hearings (although they may result from a criminal case) are civil. Suits for wrongful death are civil, as are intentional and negligent infliction of emotional distress, products liability, malpractice, and other personal and property torts and breach of contract cases. As has been repeatedly demonstrated within these pages and throughout the judiciary, many of those cases require (or could at least benefit from) utilizing the services of a forensic/consulting psychologist.

It is likely that financial considerations play a role in the perception by some that forensic psychology and litigation consulting be limited to traditional criminal matters. That type of litigation does attract the greatest media coverage and social media attention. It should be increasingly obvious to the reader that financial considerations are more likely to encourage, rather than limit, the role of psychologists in civil litigation. An increasing number of well-publicized plaintiff verdicts in excess of $10,000,000.00 reinforce that perspective.

Vinson et al. (2008) investigated the demographic and attitudinal–psychological predictors of jury verdict determinations and punitive damages in high-stakes civil litigation. Using a sophisticated and realistic research model, they determined that juror perceptions of how much of a litigation crisis existed was an effective predictor of verdict outcomes and damage awards in tobacco and pharmaceutical litigation, more so than traditional demographic variables, even after controlling for all other variables. This is a useful finding for consulting psychologists to consider in recommending appropriate voir dire questions to litigators and has significant implications for jury selection.

Arbitration Consulting

Most consulting psychologists who engage in trial consulting do it in conjunction with traditional courtroom trials. Richards (2017) noted that the American Society of Trial Consultants does not offer guidance with respect to arbitration consulting, in which consultants may also play an important role. The author recommended developing a code of conduct specific to arbitration consulting. The aspects of arbitration consulting services that are thought to be in greatest need of an ethical code of conduct include traditional witness preparation services, selection of the most favorable arbitrator (which should be a research-based determination), and small group research with respect to the various participants in the arbitration proceedings. Richards also recommended that guidelines be developed to preclude arbitration consultants from impinging on the privacy of potential arbitrators, as mock arbitration panels are developed.

SUMMARY

This chapter began by distinguishing bench trials from jury trials. In a bench trial, the judge is the sole decision maker regarding the law and facts. In a jury trial, the trier of the facts is the jury. It was noted that all criminal defendants are entitled to jury trials, and it is at their election whether a jury is actually empaneled. Assuming that in civil or criminal litigation a jury is empaneled, the remainder of the chapter explained the jury decision-making factors and the process in reaching a verdict.

4

Tools of the Forensic Consulting Trade

In the highest of high-profile litigation, attorneys wish to cover all bases. The process is, of course, expensive, but the stakes are so high that cost is rarely a primary issue. The vignette that follows describes actual litigation support attorneys engaged in for a series of related trials. The vignette and the information that follow aim to demonstrate the numerous tools available to and used by forensic consulting psychologists (FCPs) during the course of a case. In some instances, the reader might find the "tool" reference subtle or even vague. In all instances, an attempt to make the connection between the example and its function will be made.

The case description that follows includes brief mentions of many of the tools utilized for that particular case. More detailed descriptions of those and other tools follow. There may be a desire to learn more details and/or specifics about the case, but because of confidentiality agreements, certain elements were modified or disguised.

https://doi.org/10.1037/0000295-004
Forensic Organizational Consulting: The Role of Psychologists in Litigation Support, by J. M. Finkelman with L. Gomberg

VIGNETTE: THE PROCESS

The first step in the consulting process (after understanding the basic facts and legal theory of the case) is to learn as much as possible about the venue where the trial will take place. This knowledge includes demographic, occupational, financial, political, and lifestyle information about the likely juror pool. Although much of that information is available through public records, there are still gaps to be filled in at the individual prospective juror level. In order to accomplish this effectively, the litigators need to be provided with key differentiating questions to be asked during voir dire so that they may be able to determine potential juror bias and verdict predisposition (see Chapter 3).

In this case, some questions were obvious and transparent and intended to inform as to the a priori perception of possible jurors toward the attorneys' defendant-client company. But to the extent that the questions were so transparent that the opposing side fully understood their implications, that would not accomplish the main purpose of the exercise. Essentially, the questions would predict what a judge would be trying to accomplish in order to eliminate potential jurors with overt bias.

The best questions, however, are those in which the intent is not obvious to the other side or, for that matter, to the judge. Judges and opposing counsel are intelligent and, therefore, would be able to understand where the questions are leading and their probable impact on juror selection. The implication is that the underlying intent of an effective question is best if it doesn't provide too much information useful to the other sides, as well as useful for the judge. The only way this can be accomplished reliably is through research on the demographics of jurors likely to be empaneled. Research skills and interviewing techniques are essential tools of the FCP trade and need to be considered an integral component of each part of the process.

Pretrial Preparation

After learning everything we could about the composition of the potential jury pool, we recruited subjects for multiple focus groups using stratified random samples consistent with the demographics we expected to find in that pool. Our preference was to work with groups of nine to 12 participants at a time. We started with a base of questions that had been vetted and used in prior litigation that was as similar as possible to the litigation in which we were currently engaged. We refined and were able to narrow the scope of the questions after the first few focus groups. We were then able to systematically utilize those questions that seemed most revealing for subsequent focus groups.

In each such iteration, we questioned the focus group participants as to their attitude regarding the litigants and their predisposition with respect to a verdict, relating only the most superficial information about the case. In the process, we solicited information regarding both the perceived "power" and the perceived "goodness" of the defendants. Following that, the focus group facilitator shared a brief synopsis of anticipated opening statements from both plaintiffs and defendants. The final step in the initial round of focus groups was to again ask participants for a probable verdict decision, assuming they had no further information beyond the opening statements. All this information was shared, interpreted, and discussed with our clients. The objective was to determine which type of jurors to select and which to avoid, as a function of how dangerous or sympathetic their predispositions might prove to be. We tried to identify juror types that might justify expending precious peremptory challenges if they could not be eliminated for cause.

The next phase was to have the defense attorneys prepare more complete opening statement drafts for their client as well as opening statements as if they represented plaintiffs. These statements were read to focus groups sequentially in the same order they would be read in court: first by an attorney purporting to be representing plaintiffs, followed by the opening statement of the defense attorney. The participants were then surveyed with respect to how persuaded they were and for whom they were likely to vote, even though no evidence had yet been introduced. The focus group facilitator discussed their inclinations with the entire group and probed for their rationale and key decision points.

Defense attorneys unobtrusively viewed the entire focus group discussion on video from a remote location. They periodically texted the facilitator with additional questions they wanted asked in response to what they were hearing. There were multiple iterations of this process, the purpose of which was to continue refining their theory of the case, and especially their opening statements, to make their defense as compelling as possible to probable jurors.

Since cost was not a major concern in this litigation, another round of surveys and more lengthy focus groups followed, with a mock jury listening to opening arguments, simulated expert testimony, closing arguments, and then deliberating to a verdict, with defense attorneys continuing to monitor the process by video. This phase was extremely revealing to the litigators and triggered considerable discussion each evening with our litigation consulting team. Arguments and expert witness decisions were modified and tweaked accordingly.

Jury Selection

After the attorneys and judge contended with a multitude of pretrial motions beyond the scope of this volume, jury selection began. Jury consultants were in the audience gallery and surreptitiously conveyed their perspective regarding each prospective juror. In some ways, this resembled the signs that are used to convey recommendations to pitchers in major league baseball; but at trial, not only were the signals disguised, the fact they were even being delivered was concealed as well. This was accomplished in several ways, and technology played a role by which the jury consultants surreptitiously (through texting and email) gave feedback to the litigators (see Chapter 5).

In addition to real-time coaching by jury consultants in the courtroom, litigators had the benefit of significant research regarding desired juror demographics and credentials—as well as exactly the juror characteristics to avoid. Litigators were also armed with pretested voir dire questions that were facially neutral but revealed juror predispositions toward the litigants and receptivity to their tested theories of the case. Embedded consulting psychologists were also able to hear and evaluate the responses of each prospective juror and immediately convey that assessment to their attorney-clients at the defense table, typically as a simple binary yea or nay recommendation.

Experienced litigators reported afterward that the most difficult part of the process was accepting the research and recommendations of non-attorneys when either conflicted with their own seasoned instincts about jury selection. Although there is no correct answer, as with most other questions in law and psychology, the prudent response lies within the continuum of skills of both the litigator and the consulting psychologist, with the litigator remembering that the psychologist is hired for certain expertise and that much of the success of the process depends upon the way the litigator and the psychologist interact.

The visitors' gallery was quite crowded that first day of jury selection. It was a well-publicized, high-profile trial, and the press was in attendance along with the public and other interested parties. Seated unobtrusively were 14 "shadow jurors" selected to mirror the actual jury in a variety of demographic and related variables, including those that were previously determined to be associated with voting propensity. As explained earlier, stratified random sampling was used to recruit this jury.

Every evening, after court recessed for the day, the shadow jurors met with the consulting psychologists and litigation consultants at a nearby hotel that had a large suite set up to resemble a war room. Jurors were polled about all aspects of the day's trial testimony, including their impressions of the effectiveness of the attorneys on both sides, as well as the fact and expert witnesses. They were also asked to vote for a verdict, as though the trial ended at that point in time.

To say these sessions were revealing is an understatement. Many juror perceptions and votes surprised the team of attorneys and consultants. Some revelations were so significant that the litigators and associates stayed up all night refining strategy, tactics, and anticipated closing arguments. Separately, coaches were working with fact and expert witnesses to hone testimony and, in some cases, rehabilitate prior testimony that was poorly received by the mock jurors or was considered otherwise problematic.

The Verdict

This process was replicated every day of trial, and more intensive strategic and tactical discussions occurred over the weekends. The process was laborious and costly—but actually very cost-effective. Hundreds of millions of dollars were at stake. When the jury rendered a verdict for the defense, the clients were more than pleased.

Realistically, this example, although factual, was not a typical trial. As noted throughout this volume, various shortcuts can be taken to tailor the litigation consulting process to cases with lesser stakes. A certain degree of accuracy may be lost, but that need not invalidate the efficacy of the process. A cost–benefit analysis is always appropriate and commonplace with sophisticated clients and their insurance carriers, the ultimate payors.

SPECIFIC TOOLS: "SHADOW JURIES," MOCK JURIES, AND FOCUS GROUPS

Andrews (2009) credited DecisionQuest with developing the concept and coining the term "shadow jury." The use of these juries is almost ubiquitous in litigation consulting support, limited only by the considerable cost. Unlike most jury research that occurs prior to trial, shadow juries are unique in that they actually attend the trial. That presence is specifically what makes their findings so valid and useful to the litigators who engage them. The logistics are complex and need to be carefully orchestrated, precisely because the process is occurring during trial, and there is no opportunity for a do-over in the event of a mishap.

"Shadow Juries"

As was apparent from the vignette, the shadow jury permits litigators to refine arguments and redirect testimony almost in real time. This is an enormous benefit that surpasses in fidelity anything that might otherwise be utilized by consulting psychologists engaged in litigation support. Anecdotally, the shadow jurors provide positive results that cannot be achieved with other predictive instruments and techniques; no other mechanism or approach allows for the considerable advantage of continuous updating as a function of how the trial is proceeding. The relatively few consultants who have had the privilege and resources to use this technique, present company included, quickly become advocates, as do clients when costs can be justified.

It's No "Bull"

During the past several years, any discussion of shadow juries conducted with anyone who watches network television must bring to mind the CBS series *Bull* (2016–2022). Week after week, Dr. Jason Bull and his associates seem to find exact duplicates (clones?) of actual jurors selected for their trials (McGraw et al., 2016). The shadow jurors are never seen in person but are apparently hearing and/or seeing everything that goes on in the courtroom. By some miracle of technology, they even look like the actual jurors. Dr. Bull's associate monitors and transmits to him the red (anti) or green (pro) attitudes exhibited by these seeming juror avatars regarding their client. Dr. Bull is always correct in predicting which jurors should be dismissed, selected, or will come around to their client's needs. Maybe at least partially because the executive producer of the program is Dr. Phil McGraw (of Oprah Winfrey fame and daytime television), the series is not only popular but actually seems to enjoy some credibility. Of course, there is never an explanation of how the shadow jurors came to be, how they were found, or where they are specifically located (Garcia, 2017; Miller, 2019).

Who They Are

In actuality, shadow jurors are specially recruited individuals with demographics as close to the actual jurors as possible (Miller, 2019). The recruitment needs to be quick and accurate because the job of the shadow jurors requires them to sit in the courtroom all day, every day during the trial, not confer with each other, but be available to be debriefed by the consultants at least once and probably twice each day (i.e., at lunch and after the court session). Although the television show seems to have no problem finding these "doppelgängers," one can only imagine the difficulty of the task of quickly recruiting at least five to seven individuals who mirror as closely as possible the make-up of a just-selected jury and who are available to sit all day in a court for as long as the case is presented (Miller, 2019).

Mock Juries

Shelton (2006) reflected that the jury decision-making process is typically shielded from public scrutiny and social scientist oversight. We learn about it mostly through the use of mock juries, postverdict interviews, and televised documentaries. But these research methods are imprecise and subject to multiple sources of error, including sampling anomalies. Information about jury decision making is disproportionately driven by the small number of notorious trials that attract the most media attention. They are neither typical nor representative.

Shelton (2006) further contended that this selective attention interferes with the ability of juries to make complex decisions and may serve to undermine the whole jury process. Group theory identifies five specific characteristics of successful group decision making, which is analogous to the preferred jury process as follows: small size, purpose, identification, interaction, and accepted behavior. Shelton argued that court understanding of group theory or group dynamics can facilitate the jury deliberation process by moving it to a higher level of reasoning and, thus, improve the overall quality of jury decisions, the public's faith in those decisions, and the entire jury service experience. All of these are worthy objectives that can benefit from the expertise and intervention of consulting psychologists, when the legal system is sufficiently perceptive to invite their participation.

The shadow jury process, despite perfect fidelity, has little utility for advance research in preparation for jury selection and trial. Mock juries are typically used for that purpose instead. They are a step above the traditional focus group, which lacks realism and fidelity to a forthcoming trial. Focus groups are discussed more thoroughly in Chapter 1 and below. Mock juries vary significantly in their sophistication and effectiveness. Typically, they are initiated by recruiting a group of subjects who are demographically similar to what would be expected on the actual jury.

Then all or part of the anticipated trial testimony is presented to them, sometimes by the actual attorneys, sometimes by actors, and sometimes by the focus group facilitator. The more complete and accurate the case presentation is, the greater the likelihood the simulation will be representative of the actual trial and an effective research tool for the attorneys.

Many researchers assume that the results of a simple mock trial will be representative of what would occur in an actual trial, and they position their research findings accordingly. This may result in misleading conclusions and erroneous information accepted as though scientifically validated, whatever that may imply. Because it is virtually impossible to do controlled research under these circumstances, it may be a precarious assumption resulting in compromised research integrity. When mock trial results are being used to inform actual trial strategy, the consequences may be even more severe. Just as 100% accuracy in choosing sympathetic jurors is a figment of television fiction that has only a partial relationship to trial reality, so is too much reliance on the predictions of mock jurors (Miller, 2019).

Bright and Goodman-Delahunty (2011) assessed mock juror decision making in a civil negligence trial to determine the impact of gruesome evidence, injury severity, and information processing route on actual juror decision making, using first-year psychology students as subjects. Needless to say, this frequently used convenience research sample creates potential external validity issues when interpreting results, regardless of any other sources of error.

In the Bright and Goodman-Delahunty study (2011), mock jurors exposed to gruesome photographs rated the defendant as significantly more negligent than those exposed to neutral photographs, and the researchers concluded that gruesome photographic evidence could bias jurors' perceptions of the responsibility of the parties to litigation. Although that may seem logical, it is important to consider that the conclusion was based on a mock trial rather than an actual trial and the utilization of a research sample of freshman college students. Recall, however, credible meta-analysis research conducted by Bornstein et al. (2017) cited previously in this volume, suggesting that the use of student samples in mock jury or focus group research may not be all that problematic, and verdicts and awards did not vary by sample source.

Fox et al. (2011) studied jury decision making using a medical malpractice vignette as a function of participant type, either undergraduate students or jury panelists, and the apportionment of punitive damage awards as well as compensatory damages. The researchers found that overall jury panelists awarded more money for punitive damages than did the students. Jury panelists were more influenced by the details of compensatory-relevant information when making punitive-damages determinations. Jury panelists were more likely to favor the plaintiff receiving the entire punitive award, as opposed to split recovery favored by students. Unlike the Bornstein et al. (2017) meta-analysis results, Fox et al. (2011) had earlier concluded that psycholegal research conducted only with student samples may serve to misrepresent the likely behavior of actual juries, which, of course, is exactly what consulting psychologists are trying to avoid.

An inconsistent pattern is emerging in which some studies suggest that sample composition in this type of litigation-related research is less critical than we might have anticipated, while other research reflects significant and meaningful differences as a direct function of the participants being surveyed or observed. The salient factors for consulting psychologists are that external validity and the fidelity of simulation are pivotal determinants of the integrity and utility of actionable research.

With respect to mock jury research, Wiener et al. (2011) reviewed the four types of validity that make up the usual approach to research in the social sciences, and they focused on the following dimensions of psychological research: internal validity, external validity, and construct validity. They determined that the most significant impediment to the generalizability of jury research was the interaction of the sample with elements of construct validity, rather than any reliance on undergraduate students as mock jurors, as had been speculated.

The concern was that student mock jurors might react differently in a simulated trial than subjects who were more representative of jurors in a given venue. Wiener et al. (2011) called for a two-stage research process:

Findings obtained with a convenience sample could form the basis for a second stage in which more realistic trial processes are added and more representative research samples are used. This would enable researchers to validate those findings and thus increase the fidelity and credibility the research and consequently the veracity of the outcome.

Solnik (2006) explained the role of mock juries most succinctly: They offer a trial run for savvy lawyers. The author readily acknowledged that the facts are the facts, and facts cannot be changed. Rather litigators and their consultants "have to understand [that perception] is the filter that human beings use to translate those facts" (Solnik, 2006, p. 1). To paraphrase Solnik's advice: It's better to lose with the preshow and win the main event.

Focusing on Focus Groups

Basic focus group research has commonly been used since the 1960s, and the underlying principles and techniques have changed little. It is a very adaptable process that, in large measure, accounts for its continuing popularity. Focus group research can be implemented simply and inexpensively or in a more complex and costly fashion, depending on the objective of the research. The focus groups that consulting psychologists typically employ in litigation support tend toward the more complex and costly end of the continuum. That is because they need to be customized to the parameters of each trial in order to maximize their effectiveness and predictive validity.

Greenbaum (1998) advocated an issue-oriented approach for application to litigation. Participant subjects were recruited to resemble as closely as possible the demographics and psychographics of the juror pool in the trial venue. The process of this approach was estimated to take an average of about 2.5 hours. In my experience, participants begin to lose focus and thus accuracy beyond that time frame. This can be an issue in the actual trial as well, as litigators struggle to hold the attention of the jury. The focus group participants are first exposed to an overview of the case and the most salient factors that may have precipitated the trial. This is followed by a synopsis of the main arguments that the plaintiff and defense attorneys are expected to advance. Typically, two people present these summaries, one of whom may be the actual litigator and the other an attorney or actor portraying opposing counsel. Focus group participants cannot know which side represents the actual client who engaged the research.

In using Greenbaum's (1998) approach, the participants are asked to write a brief summary of what they heard, indicating the most salient points made by each side and their impressions of the presenters. This process commits them to a position before being influenced by others in the focus group. Then the moderator leads a discussion about the strengths of the case and the relative effectiveness of the arguments from both sides. Greenbaum maintained that the issue-oriented approach is most helpful after a mock trial has been conducted, so litigators gain information about the most persuasive issues in their case. The process can be repeated as often as necessary to further refine arguments if litigation budgets and insurance carriers permit.

Focus groups have become increasingly more common in civil and criminal litigation, although litigators are often satisfied with the results of as few as two such groups to assist their trial preparation. Typically, the number of groups is a function of the financial stakes at trial and the complexity of the issues that will guide the process.

APPLYING THE TOOLS

No description of the tools of the consulting psychology trade would be complete, or even very helpful, if it didn't include the application of those tools and/or some viable and updated alternatives to those tools.

Electronic Alternatives to Voir Dire

There is a ready market for rapid and inexpensive alternatives to traditional voir dire, although no one approach has gained widespread acceptance among litigators. No such technique is likely to replace the final questioning of potential jurors by attorneys and judges, but there are ways to accelerate the process through computer-aided search protocols that can be initiated prior to questioning any prospective jurors. This tool could permit attorneys to spend their limited voir dire time in search of more abstract dimensions of prospective juror biases and predispositions. It is commonplace for consultants to simply search the internet for the names of each potential juror. Although that occasionally results in useful qualifying information, it could also result in name confusion and misinformation if the researcher isn't scrupulously careful.

In his 2017 article, Carlson advocated for available software that claims to search billions of data points within moments and tap public records as well as social media posts about prospective jurors; it then generates customized reports that can be viewed on a laptop or smartphone. The process has enjoyed some measure of success since being introduced in 2015. It can be used by litigators directly, but it may be more productive in the hands of consulting psychologists who can integrate results within a broader framework of predictive information and even develop appropriate follow-up questions to be asked during voir dire, based on what has been uncovered in the search. It is likely that competitive software programs are already in development with similar objectives. It is even reasonable to expect apps that are readily available for download to altogether bypass the need for customized reports, although consulting psychologists are unlikely to be replaced by smartphones anytime soon.

Ryan (2010) took the position that "the civil jury trials in both state and federal courts are rapidly going the way of the dodo" (p. 425), in large measure because of the skyrocketing costs of trial and the preceding discovery process. Ryan maintained that costs are why so many defendants are willing to pay extortionist size settlements rather than take the case to trial. Electronic alternatives to voir dire are among the several approaches that are being advanced to control costs and that could benefit from the guidance of consulting psychologists. Ryan argued that cost controls will be necessary if jury trials are to survive. Although that may have been a bit of an overstatement, even in 2010, the trend was clear.

Jury Selection Bias

Joy and McMunigal (2016) referenced the 1875 Civil Rights Act as the likely origin of concerns about racial discrimination in jury selection within the U.S. criminal justice system. Recalling that the 13th Amendment to the U.S. Constitution (which ended "involuntary servitude") had been ratified only 10 years prior to that Act, African American jurors were customarily and legally excluded from juries. The problem subsequent to the 1875 Civil Rights Act—and all subsequent Civil Rights Acts—is that the same nefarious objectives can be accomplished by unethical attorneys including prosecutors through the misuse of peremptory challenges, making the prejudice difficult to detect and preclude. Peremptory challenges have legitimate value, under the law, but can be readily misused. As was discussed in Chapter 2, the law is consistently attempting to end this not-so-subtle practice. *Batson-Wheeler* or *Batson* objections can be made during trial, on appeal, and in civil or criminal cases (Draft Memo Re *Batson-Wheeler* Motions, n.d.). Attorneys (perhaps with the help of the consulting psychologist) need to be alert to the misuse by others and avoid even the appearance of bias on their own part.

Litigators and their attorneys, of course, attempt to reject or challenge jurors they anticipate will be averse to their theory of the case. To the extent that adverse jurors respond to voir dire in a manner that demonstrates an overt prejudice for or against either side, the judge will likely strike those individuals, or one of the attorneys will move to strike for cause (there is no limit to challenges for cause). Most jury selection challenges are far less obvious, and the judge decides whether there are sufficient grounds to strike a prospective juror. There is nothing improper when attorneys attempt to get rid of adverse jurors using their peremptory challenges— unless the basis for the challenge appears to be discriminatory animus or due to membership in a protected group. This is where it gets tricky. How do judges determine underlying motive? As discussed in Chapter 2, upon motion by a party, the judge has the complex task of determining the motivation of the challenged party. Although case law on the subject has continued to refine and evolve the use of the *Batson-Wheeler* motion over the decades, those specifics are beyond the scope of this volume.

In a revealing study, Clark et al. (2007) tested the use of the five-factor model of personality traits as a predictor of jury selection and jury decision making, using the established Big Five Inventory in both civil and criminal cases. Somewhat surprisingly, although jury selection decisions were not associated with the measured personality traits, they were associated with the race and gender of the jurors. This is problematic because both race and gender are considered protected categories and cannot be the basis for a decision to strike a juror. This finding raises obvious strategic and tactical issues for attorneys. They may anticipate that jurors of a certain gender or race are likely to be predisposed for or against their clients. They may even have research supporting that concern. But using those factors as the basis for selecting jurors is not acceptable. Attorneys are obligated to come up with persuasive alternative justification to support eliminating a potential juror when they can't find cause.

Cover (2017) effectively captured the dilemma as follows: "Modern jury selection is pulled in two directions. Equal protection prohibits racial discrimination, but the traditional peremptory strike permits exclusion of a juror without explanation" (p. 357). Cover explained that to reconcile this tension, the "*Batson* framework" was developed, which upon motion requires lawyers to explain what she calls ex-post-race-neutral justifications for suspicious strikes. The problem remains that even after almost 4 decades, its effectiveness in uncovering latent discrimination has not been firmly established.

Cover (2017) argued that the systemic persistence of discrimination, decades after the *Batson* challenge became available, convinced many that the real solution is to eliminate peremptory strikes; she does offer an alternative process for reform that she calls the hybrid jury strike. "Hybrid strikes would fall in between traditional peremptory challenges, which may be exercised at the party's discretion, and challenges for cause, which may be granted only upon an adequate showing of juror bias or other basis for disqualification" (p. 357).

Although the U.S. Supreme Court precludes attorneys from considering the protected status characteristics, including the race and gender of prospective jurors, as the basis for peremptory challenges, M. I. Norton et al. (2007) are more inflexible in supporting challenges not demanding any justification. The researchers proposed that forbidding peremptory strikes based on social category information would not only fail to decrease biased jury selection, "but also encourages attorneys to search—successfully—for neutral justifications for their biased decisions" (p. 467).

It was noteworthy that some research subjects, acting in the role of prosecutor in a jury selection simulation, struck female prospective jurors more frequently than male jurors and defended these discriminatory selections claiming gender-neutral rationales.

Peremptory Strikes and the Consulting Psychologists

As has been and will continue to be seen, much has been written about the discriminatory potential of the unregulated and excessive use of peremptory strikes to minimize or eliminate protected group representation on a jury. These strikes continue to be controversial, and consulting psychologists are often put in the position of having to recommend their use to serve the best interests of their clients. Leshem (2019) noted that critics have called for their elimination following the *Batson v. Kentucky* (1986) decision, because of their continued misuse. But defenders point to the impartiality these strikes represent. Aside from the availability of the *Batson-Wheeler* motion (*Batson* in federal court), the use of peremptory challenges has frequently been criticized and equally as often been defended for other reasons.

Leshem (2019) argued that peremptory strikes also serve in the interest of democratic legitimacy, noting that the selection of jurors is analogous to the election of political representatives, which provides a check against the state's coercive power. Leshem advocated for allocating different numbers of peremptory strikes depending upon the case(s) and jury size.

These reforms seem to make sense from the perspective of consulting psychologists engaged in litigation support, because they serve to better protect against discriminatory abuse while permitting the flexibility to make recommendations that allow for professional judgment calls to protect against selecting jurors who are biased for or against a litigant before ever hearing the facts and issues in the case—completely unrelated to protected status. Thus, consulting psychologists can operate ethically and effectively with sufficient degrees of freedom to make a meaningful contribution at trial.

Diversity in Jury Selection and the Evolving Limitations on Peremptory Challenges

Afanador (2018) noted that the Sixth and Seventh Amendments to the U.S. Constitution do not guarantee that a litigant is entitled to a diverse jury or a jury of peers but rather only to an impartial jury. Although racial diversity may be a noble goal, it is not a legal right. However, there is considerable racial diversity scrutiny, and lawyers are restricted in how they elect to exclude potential jurors. It is often challenging to differentiate legitimate from nefarious motives in jury selection and the exercise of peremptory challenges. This makes it paramount for consulting psychologists engaged in jury selection to be cautious and aware of diversity issues, as well as appearances, throughout the selection process. They may elect to be proactive and test peremptory challenges using a derivation of a statistical adverse impact analysis with respect to both juror gender and juror race.

Considering the *Batson* framework of sensitivity to discrimination to which attorneys must adhere, Afanador (2018) argued that the lawyers conducting the Bill Cosby 2017 sexual assault trial would have been well advised to focus on a clear unbiased rationale for striking potential jurors, without forfeiting their objective to achieve a racially diverse jury or undermining their theory of the case. It seems apparent that attorneys and their jury consultants will need to prepare for greater scrutiny in the way they conduct voir dire and be able to defend peremptory strikes with empirical evidence of bias. Diverse juries and selection pools are probably advantageous for all parties. Afanador pondered "whether being too sensitive to diversity is an asset or a detriment" (p. 58).

The *Daubert* Test and the Consulting Psychologist

Wingate and Thornton (2004) explored judicial perceptions of the field of industrial and organizational (I/O) psychology by surveying how federal judges evaluate I/O expert witness testimony. They reviewed federal judges' use of the *Daubert* standard in their admissions decisions (see Chapter 2, this volume). One hundred fifty federal judges (approximately 10% of the randomly selected) population responded and were randomly presented with different prototypical descriptions of I/O psychology expert witness testimony in age discrimination in civil employment litigation. These judges were generally not conversant with the field of I/O psychology, and not many had even heard or read the testimony of an I/O psychologist. Still, two thirds of responders said they were at least moderately likely to admit an I/O expert's testimony at trial.

The federal judges rated evidence as relevant, moderately reliable, moderately probative, or prejudicial. Wingate and Thornton (2004) found familiarity with the field of I/O psychology and prior experience with I/O testimony to be positively related to the likelihood of admitting I/O evidence. Surprisingly, the scientific foundation for the expert testimony did not substantially affect the judges' admission decisions. They ascribed the greatest importance to what the researchers termed the "general acceptance *Daubert* factor" (Wingate & Thornton, 2004, p. 108).

Although *Daubert v. Merrell Dow Pharmaceuticals, Inc.* (1993) is thoroughly discussed in Chapter 2, this finding by these researchers bears some discussion. Eleven years after the *Daubert* decision, it seemed as if the abandoned phrase "general acceptance" continued to trigger a positive response on the part of federal judges (*Frye v. United States*, 1923). What Wingate and Thornton (2004) had done was to rephrase the four factors of the *Daubert* standard into testability, peer, review, error rate, and general acceptance, which was the researchers' term for reliability (FRE 702, 2021; see also Chapter 1, this volume). Basically, the responses showed a lack of scientific concern for admitting expert testimony, which could well have been exactly what the *Daubert* dissenters feared when they stated that judges were not scientists, and giving them such discretion on admissibility of scientific evidence put too much of a burden on them as gatekeepers (*Daubert v. Merrell Dow Pharmaceuticals, Inc.*, 1993; see also Chapter 1, this volume). However, one must keep in mind that generally, and as stated earlier, all relevant evidence is admissible (FRE 402, 2021). Assuming proffered expert testimony is relevant, the judge's only decision on admissibility, according to the FRE, *Daubert*, and the progeny of *Daubert*, is whether the evidence is reliable. Based on that reasoning and the fact that there's probably much more chance of a judge being reversed on appeal if evidence is excluded rather that admitted, the judge would logically be more prone to allowing the testimony than not.

Witness Preparation

It is rare to encounter an attorney who does not believe that witness preparation is essential (see Chapter 1). Many attorneys elect to do it themselves, whereas some have the resources to explore and understand the utility of engaging a consulting psychologist or a professional witness coach. There is little question that attorneys know their cases best, but there is a real issue as to whether attorneys also possess the skill set necessary to prepare witnesses regarding the most credible and persuasive delivery style, including the frequently overlooked aspect of nonverbal communication. It is useful to separate the two components of witness preparation—content and style.

In my experience, attorneys are best at the former, whereas consultants are better at the latter. As previously mentioned, ethical issues may be raised when an attorney or preparation consultant attempts to alter the content of the testimony rather than the style in which it is presented. Of course, it is always appropriate for an attorney to remind witnesses about the facts of a case, unless they are fact witnesses who will be called upon for precisely that recollection. Expert witnesses, however, in particular, may need their recollection of the facts of a case refreshed because that aspect is likely to be independent of their expertise.

Boccaccini (2002) lamented that although social scientists know a great deal about communication skills and persuasion, there has been a lack of research to learn whether these qualities can be enhanced through witness preparation training. Until that happens, we may only be speculating as to the likelihood of change and, therefore, doing a great deal of witness preparation without an empirical understanding of its true effectiveness or the differential utility of the various approaches being used.

Another aspect of witness preparation may be as simple as coaching in nonverbal communication such as smiling while on the witness stand.

It is known that women, in general, smile more frequently than men. Nagle et al. (2014) investigated the influence of facial expressions, such as smiling, on perceived credibility of real testifying witnesses at trial.

"Credibility raters" assessed trustworthiness, level of confidence, knowledgeability, likeability, and total credibility of subjects, using the "Witness Credibility Scale." These rated qualities were compared with the manner and frequency of witness smiling behavior. Gender was found to be correlated with trustworthiness, with men perceived as more trustworthy than women, despite the absence of a disparity in how often they smiled. However, Nagle et al. (2014) concluded that smiling in general was a significant determinant of likeability, quite independent of gender, although smiling women were favored over both smiling men and women who did not smile.

Nagle et al. (2014) concluded that nonverbal communication, such as smiling, in real witnesses testifying at actual trials did influence subsequent ratings of witness credibility, although the magnitude of credibility varied somewhat by gender. Consulting psychologists engaged in witness preparation activities can use these findings as well as other forms of nonverbal witness communication behavior to help coach witnesses to be more appealing and credible on the witness stand.

Making the Case

Forsterlee et al. (2005) used an elaborate mock trial involving multiple plaintiffs and expert witnesses to assess the effect of various cognitive aids, such as providing summary statements of expert scientific witnesses on quality of juror decision making and size of verdict in a civil trial. The researchers found that the combination of summary statements and note-taking by mock jurors had a synergistic effect on decision making, such that the cognitively aided jurors awarded more money to the most severely injured plaintiffs, but the aids did not alter their awards to plaintiffs with less severe injuries. Aided jurors also recalled more probative evidence than their nonaided counterparts. These are significant findings for consulting psychologists trying to enhance the effectiveness of witness testimony for either party to the litigation.

Influencing Trial Outcomes: Opening Statements and Closing Arguments

It is obviously useful to be able to predict trial outcomes, but it is even more compelling for litigators to be able to influence trial verdicts and awards. Consulting psychologists have an important contribution to make in both circumstances. Spiecker and Worthington (2003) examined the influence of the organizational strategy used to structure opening statements and closing arguments on presentation effectiveness in a simulated civil trial. The researchers found that a mixed organizational strategy, with a narrative opening and a legal-expository closing, was more effective for the plaintiff than a strict narrative strategy, and either a mixed or strict legal-expository strategy was more effective for the defense.

Litigation consultants as well as legal communication scholars have long recognized the critical importance of opening statements and closing arguments in juror decision making (Matlon, 1988; Rieke & Stutman, 1990). Some litigators have maintained that lawsuits can be won or lost in the opening statement (Connolly, 1982). Research dating back to the 1980s demonstrates the importance of opening statements, because they create the framework through which jurors filter all subsequent evidence that is presented at trial (Moore, 1989; Pyszczynski & Wrightsman, 1981).

In a similar vein, closing arguments are persuasive due to their ability to synthesize trial information and remind jurors of evidence that litigators believe to be pivotal to establishing their case (Matlon, 1988). Although the ostensible purpose of a closing argument is "to facilitate the jury's proper analysis of the evidence presented at trial so that it may arrive at a just and reasonable conclusion based on the evidence alone and not on any fact not admitted into evidence" (Montz, 2001, p. 73), Montz (2001) reminded us of the reality that litigators typically view closing arguments as their last and best chance to convince the jury of their interpretation of the evidence and the law, in a way that is most consistent with their theory of the case and most likely to result in a favorable verdict.

As in so many other instances described in this book, consulting psychologists can play a pivotal role in helping litigators both formulate and test the efficacy of their opening statements and closing arguments. This is where experimental rigor and science can support the art and practice of litigation.

APPLYING THE SCIENCE

Lecci and Myers (2008) explored the constructs that were associated with attitudinal differences among potential jurors and validated their findings with a confirmatory factor analysis. They determined that the highly regarded Pretrial Juror Attitude Questionnaire (PJAQ) provided superior predictivity for potential juror bias than other methods more often used to accomplish this.

Lecci and Myers (2008) determined that the PJAQ can accurately assess conviction proneness, confidence in the judicial system, cynicism directed at the litigants, racial bias, and even innate criminality within potential jurors. The scales should be useful for consulting psychologists seeking to understand jury decision making, detect bias, and perhaps even predict trial outcomes. It is the rigorous methodology and underlying empirical approach that accounts for the popularity and value of the PJAQ, and it sets the standard for subsequent instruments and the creation of new predictive constructs that will assist litigation consultants well into the future.

Scientific Jury Selection

Scientific jury selection (SJS) refers to the use of social science techniques, methodologies, and expertise to select potential jurors who are favorably disposed to support their theory and position during a criminal or civil trial (Vinson et al., 2008). Psychologists and social scientists have been assisting litigators in a variety of capacities for many decades. The original entry point was jury selection, but that eventually expanded to a more focused prediction of trial outcomes and the testing of trial strategy and tactics, as well as opening and closing arguments. Although SJS has become almost ubiquitous in high-stakes and high-profile civil litigation by both plaintiff and defense attorneys, it is consistently being extended to lower profile litigation. The reason is that it works and has become more cost-effective to use. The accuracy of some of these techniques, grounded in real science, can be quite extraordinary.

The concept of SJS has been gaining increasing traction with litigators seeking to gain a competitive advantage at trial based on the composition and demeanor of the jury (see Chapter 1). This would be in addition to the facts and issues associated with their theory of the case, over which they may feel greater confidence and control. As such, it becomes a form of added insurance that may serve to their advantage or at least reduce the likelihood of an unjustified adverse outcome. Hence, one realizes the popularity of using scientifically trained consulting psychologists as jury selection consultants.

Lieberman (2011) observed that these consultants typically use a variety of survey and observational approaches based on purportedly rigorous research techniques to conduct SJS research, sometimes during actual trials; consultants use these approaches to determine the relationship between background characteristics of jurors and their inclinations to either convict or acquit a criminal defendant. Lieberman reviewed many instances of this type of research and concluded that although SJS may have some merit, methodological flaws often preclude clear conclusions. The author correctly argued for higher quality, evaluative research.

This argument creates an obvious opportunity for consulting psychologists who have the skill and training to do exactly that—and thereby distinguish themselves from pseudo-SJS practitioners who do not have the requisite experience and scientific rigor to be able to reliably accomplish what they claim to be able to do. The proof is in the accuracy of jury selection recommendations—or the lack thereof. The implication is that Lieberman's (2011) skepticism may be based on a sample of widely varying credentials and experience, on behalf of practitioners making similar SJS representations.

Seltzer (2006) reminded us that early efforts at SJS were often engaged to guide the exercise of peremptory challenges (see this chapter and elsewhere in this volume). Political trials (e.g., those resulting from the Attica Prison Riots, the Harrisburg Seven antiwar activists, the Battle of Wounded

Knee) in the early 1970s were among the first to use social science to help attorneys select juries (McConahay et al., 1977; Schulman et al., 1973). Although early SJS concentrated on the use of demographic character-istics to predict jury verdicts, the focus now is on developing a theory of the case, which shapes the strategy for jury selection. The original mass opinion surveys have largely been replaced by more sophisticated trial simulations or at least by professionally conducted focus groups.

Seltzer (2006) anticipated the trend that has persisted for the decades since—to have SJS expand into a multimillion-dollar industry serving wealthy litigators and even public defenders. In his article, Seltzer refer-enced the classic high-profile trials of O. J. Simpson, the Menendez brothers, Martha Stewart, the first Rodney King trial, the William Kennedy Smith rape trial, and the $1 million McDonald's verdict. Not surprisingly, Seltzer concluded that the type of case being tried determines to some extent the efficacy of SJS.

Juror Questions

Finally, although some might argue that there's nothing scientific about allowing jurors to ask questions of witnesses, in 2012, the Illinois Supreme Court followed the lead of other state courts and instituted its Rule 243—the Rule allows just that (Thies, 2013). Although some attorneys were con-cerned that the questions would take too much time, be irrelevant, or be inappropriate, experience proved that not to be the case. In the states that allow jurors to ask questions in civil cases, only about one third did so, and the questions (on average of only 2.5) were appropriate and added merely 10 minutes to the total length of the trial. Permitting jurors to propose questions to witnesses, however, is still not common in civil courts, but when requested and granted (at the discretion of the judge), the situation provides some unique opportunities for consulting psychologists serving as litigation consultants.

Rose et al. (2006) characterized the questioning as a potentially valuable tool for jurors as well as a window into juror thinking. It is the latter func-tion that offers the best opportunity for litigation support by psychologists because of the unique insights the questions may be able to offer, based on the types of questions that are being advanced and how they are positioned, regarding the verdict inclination of jurors. Settlements during trial can be informed and triggered by the questions advanced by the jury. The questions have a meaning that transcends the information being solicited and should be interpreted as such.

Rose et al. (2006) examined questions that jurors submitted during 50 civil trials and analyzed the videotapes of jury deliberations in those cases. The researchers reported that the overwhelming majority of juror questions demonstrated a problem-solving approach that was consistent with their role as factfinders, rather than as advocates. They noted that the procedures used to guide the questioning process can be crucial in establishing their effectiveness. Consulting psychologists can maximize the utility and interpretability of juror questions.

SUMMARY

Although not all tools of the forensic consulting trade are tangible or even precisely definable, this chapter brought together and described the tools and skills necessary for an effective FCP to utilize. Overarching all the other tools is research skill. Researching every issue in each case is mandatory. Shadow juries, mock juries, and focus groups are among the specific tools frequently employed. In fact, popular television illuminates the use of such tools with shows such as the weekly series *Bull*. This chapter also provided other examples of these tools and their application by describing a true case vignette and highly publicized trials.

5

Posttrial Consultation

Sometimes it is only after the trial is over that all the elements can be dissected, carefully reviewed, and their value assessed. Fortunately, there's always another trial, and what has been learned in retrospect comes together to be applied to and help that next trial make sense. Various components and topics that were discussed may be seen from a different perspective; some topics that may have been overlooked take on more prominence after the fact. Certain commonalities become apparent in specific types of litigation, and there are even times when casual conversation, socializing, and/or directed debriefing among the litigation team members help clarify, win or lose, what transpired during the process.

https://doi.org/10.1037/0000295-005
Forensic Organizational Consulting: The Role of Psychologists in Litigation Support, by J. M. Finkelman with L. Gomberg

THE JURY AND THE JURORS

Jury decision-making biases and distortions are problematic and well known within the legal community (see Chapter 3). Although researchers have struggled to understand the problem, litigators and litigation consultants have been more focused on turning these biases to their advantage. Daftary-Kapur et al. (2010) summarized the state of the process, noting that, despite more than 50 years of scientific research on juries and jury decision making, legal scholars have not gained a complete understanding of factors that can have an untoward influence on juries. The authors reviewed the spectrum of biases associated with jury decision making; these included the impact of pretrial publicity, jury instructions, inadvertently hearing inadmissible evidence, and scientific evidence.

With respect to jury instructions, their research demonstrated that jurors have difficulties understanding standardized instructions. Daftary-Kapur et al. (2010) suggested ways instructions can be rewritten to increase comprehensibility. Regarding inadmissible evidence, the authors acknowledged the cognitive effort involved in attempting to disregard evidence, but no clear strategy emerged as to how to eliminate the associated problems. Lack of comprehension of scientific evidence has no quick fix other than better education of jurors and judges. Finally, the threats posed by pretrial publicity to the defendant's right to a fair trial are clear—but a cost-effective solution is not, including the complex change of venue option to help overcome local media-induced biases.

Although the following may be related to the work of the consulting psychologist in only the most peripheral way, its relevance to the importance and interpretation of jury instructions is illuminating. In 2013 in Florida, a White man named George Zimmerman shot and killed a 16-year-old Black youth named Trayvon Martin. As a sort of neighborhood watch vigilante, Zimmerman noticed the boy walking through the community on his way home. When Zimmerman called authorities because he was (for some reason that probably had to do with racism) suspicious that the boy was up to no good, the authorities told Zimmerman to go home. Instead, he followed and accosted the boy. They fought; Zimmerman, a very large man, ended up on his back on the cement walk with Martin on top of him. George Zimmerman took out his gun and shot and killed Trayvon Martin; Zimmerman was subsequently tried for second-degree murder and the lesser included crime of manslaughter. He pled self-defense. When the all-female jurors deliberated Zimmerman's guilt, they did so after having been read 27 pages of jury instructions (Kelley, 2013). Their verdict of not guilty was met with anger and confusion by most of the general public (Bates, 2013). However, during the trial, Zimmerman's attorney had brought in a large slab of concrete stating (and pounding) that Martin had continually slammed the back of the defendant's head onto the concrete. Zimmerman had the lacerations to prove the injuries. Among the 27 pages was this instruction: "A person is justified in using deadly force if he reasonably believes that such force is necessary to prevent imminent death or great bodily harm to himself" (Kelley, 2013, para. 27). The defense attorney's courtroom drama convinced the jury that Zimmerman was, in fact, trying to prevent his own "imminent death" when he shot Martin. Further, Zimmerman was legally where he was and had a licensed gun. The instructions made clear that Florida law expressly stated the defendant had a right to stand his ground if he felt threatened (Kelley, 2013). Zimmerman's prior behavior was not included in the instructions.

Influence of Voir Dire

Recalling once again that voir dire is the questioning process used by attorneys and judges prior to empaneling a juror, consulting psychologists recognize that voir dire questions can be used to surreptitiously influence jurors' perception of the case and inoculate them against anticipated unfavorable information that may be contrary to their theory of the case. Essentially, the jury can be sensitized and programmed as to how to interpret subsequent case-related content in such a way as to change their initial perception of the case. At least that is the hope of the side engaging in this often-transparent manipulation.

Greathouse et al. (2011) examined voir dire questions in transcripts from trials in which juveniles would be tried as adults. They readily concluded that the influence of the questions created a more conviction-prone jury. In other words, if potential jurors could or would not agree that juveniles could or should be tried as adults, they were excused for cause. The researchers realized many of the questions were similar to those asked when trying to establish a death-qualified jury, which they also found to be conviction prone. What they found after their three studies was that the conviction proneness caused by death-qualification voir dire also occurred in juvenile-qualification voir dire. In other words, they found that participants who viewed a juvenile-qualification voir dire were more likely to agree that the defendant was guilty and would be convicted than participants who viewed a standard voir dire that did not contain juvenile-qualification questions. The researchers noted that this outcome was like findings in the death-qualification literature, suggesting that when jurors are asked to consider sentencing a defendant before being exposed to actual trial evidence, they are more prone to be predisposed against the defendant.

The researchers ultimately concluded that although juvenile-qualification questions may create pretrial prejudice against a defendant, the bias may not be sufficient to alter posttrial the perceptions of guilt at the conclusion of the trial. Mock jurors' posttrial verdict determinations were almost exclusively influenced by the strength of the trial evidence. The findings challenged whether other types of pretrial biases are diminished by trial evidence, including pretrial biases induced through capital voir dire procedures. Greathouse et al. (2011) maintained, however, that despite the death-qualification process influencing other aspects of capital jury decision making, their results cast doubt on whether merely exposing jurors to the types of questions asked in death-qualifying voir dire actually resulted in a greater number of convictions.

Although the case and 2020 appeal of Dzhokhar A. Tsarnaev (known as the Boston Marathon Bomber) is discussed in Chapter 6 in its relevance to the issue of social media in the courts, some of the discussion in the 234-page opinion also is relevant to any discussion of voir dire. Much of that opinion is devoted to a thorough and relevant discussion of voir dire and its importance in jury selection (*United States v. Tsarnaev*, 2013). Apparently, because of the enormous amount of negative publicity prior to the trial, the defense counsel had asked for a change of venue (four times) and for special questions to be asked of potential jurors during voir dire. The judge consistently denied the change of venue and the list of special questions but did "promise to conduct a thorough and searching voir dire" (*United States v. Tsarnaev*, 2013, p. 19). In that case, the same jury sat for both the guilt and penalty phases of the proceedings.

Looking at the numbers of potential jurors originally summoned and eventually narrowed might give some context to the complexity of jury selection in the *Tsarnaev* case. Originally, 1,373 individuals were summoned and filled out questionnaires as to their suitability to sit on a jury that might result in a death sentence, if the defendant was found guilty. After review by both sides, 256 of them were retained to undergo individual voir dire. The judge had calendared 21 days for this process. During this period, the defendant continued to request that the judge ask certain questions of the potential jurors and continued to seek a change of venue. Both requests were denied.

At the end of the 21 days, the jury pool consisted of 75 potential jurors. One of the 181 who had been excused was a criminal defense attorney who admitted he had a difficult time with the death penalty (this was among the 16 issues raised at the appeal). He did, however, state that, given certain circumstances the potential juror believed he could vote for it. The prosecution moved that he be stricken for cause. The defense, of course, found him completely acceptable. The judge dismissed the individual because the "sense of him" caused the judge to determine he wouldn't be "truly open" to the death penalty (*United States v. Tsarnaev*, 2013). As the pool went from 75 to 70 and eventually to the 12 jurors who actually sat on the trial, the defense continually asked for a change of venue and repeatedly asked that two other jurors be removed. The implication was that the excused juror's responses should not have been reason to excuse him, and voir dire had not been sufficient to expose reasons the two other jurors should have been excused. As will be seen in Chapter 5, this would be determined later to be judicial error and abuse of discretion.

Mulvaney and Litter (2015) stressed the criticality of the entire voir dire process, for reasons similar to those advanced herein—"that a case may be won or lost before opening statements based solely on the composition of the jury" (p. 313). Considering that perspective, Mulvaney and Litter lamented that, given its influence on a verdict determination at trial, lawyers don't put as much research and effort into jury selection as it may warrant. Although voir dire guidelines vary greatly by jurisdiction, consulting psychologists can help lawyers maximize whatever opportunities exist for questioning prospective jurors. Perhaps the most essential support they can provide is to identify those jurors who are too dangerous to their client or to their theory of the case to be allowed to serve.

Lee (2015) acknowledged that opinions differ on whether it is advisable to question jurors as to their racial bias proclivity during voir dire. Although jurors may be unlikely to acknowledge (or even be aware of) their bias, Lee concluded that racial bias can still be diminished by asking relevant questions to prospective jurors during voir dire (*United States v. Tsarnaev*, 2020). The perspective is that by alerting potential jurors to the indecency of racial bias, the concern can become more relevant to the jury and consequently minimize such misbehavior.

Story-Mediated Models in Civil Litigation

Jurors, as most members of society are known to do, use their personal experiences to interpret information they learn at trial to construct stories that help them reach a verdict determination. Much of the research regarding this has been conducted in conjunction with criminal litigation, with strong empirical support. Huntley and Costanzo (2003) tested a story-mediated model and an unmediated model of juror responses to sexual harassment litigation. Path analyses supported the story-mediated model, which accounted for significant variance in the verdict outcome measures of juror decision making.

Those determined to be pro plaintiff or pro defense jurors used very different stories to explain the same case. The researchers noted that sexual harassment cases may be unique because of drama in mass media coverage and the inherent interest of the public in anything that has to do with sex. Certainly, at least for the most part, jurors would have more familiarity with and interest in the work settings in which such conduct occurs than they would with other types of cases (e.g., breach of contract). Not surprisingly, gender was the only juror characteristic that was consistently related to final verdicts, in large measure because of the typical genders (male harassing female) of the two parties in sexual harassment, although that stereotype is changing and evolving. The mediated relationship between gender and verdict suggests that gender affected which story version jurors endorsed. Overall, consistent with prior research, there was a relatively weak relationship between other juror characteristics and verdict outcomes.

Consulting psychologists should appreciate that the research focused only on themes that divided the jurors. Huntley and Costanzo (2003) observed that jurors on both sides of a case do not answer all theme-related questions in a noticeably different way, suggesting that jurors create stories before they reach a verdict. Had that not been the case, we might anticipate that jurors on opposite sides would answer each theme-related question in a way most favorable to the side they supported. The implication for future research and for consulting psychologists serving as litigation consultants is that there is utility in assessing jurors' prototypes before they hear a case.

This type of assessment could permit an understanding of how juror predispositions shape the interpretation of trial evidence, which would be of enormous value to litigators. The goal would be to determine juror predispositions and predict their interpretations using researched and targeted voir dire questions (assuming that, unlike the judge in the case above, the parties were allowed to use the questions). Consulting psychologists are in a unique position to do that credibly and ethically to assist litigators in developing case theories and trial tactics that resonate with the triers of fact.

Predicting Jury Verdicts: Value of Second Opinions

Consulting psychologists can serve the interests of litigators by sharing the research regarding the utility of aggregating the opinions of colleagues and creating the methodology that permits them to do this in a rigorous fashion, while at the same time attributing proper weight to alternative perspectives. Although trial attorneys often seek second opinions from other attorneys as to probable jury verdicts prior to accepting a case, especially on the plaintiff side, consulting psychologists need to be aware that this is one more service they can provide for their employer (see Chapter 3).

Jacobson et al. (2011) conducted research trying to determine how effectively attorneys used second opinions after they were solicited or offered. They found that when attorneys were given access to a partner's estimates, their accuracy improved. However, attorneys typically underweighted their partners' estimates relative to their own, with experienced attorneys giving less weight to their partners' opinions than did law students participating in the research. Jacobson and colleagues strongly recommended that attorneys seek out a second opinion and give that opinion more weight than they might initially be inclined to do.

Mathie (2016) advised that mediation provides attorneys another chance to assess the worth of a case. The author noted that the opinion derived from mediation will be from a different perspective than their own estimate or from one that is solicited from colleagues. An arithmetic average of the various estimates is likely to be closer to what the jury verdict is likely to be, than is any one estimate, especially if it is the extreme high or low amount. It is the safest route for an attorney seeking the most realistic assessment of the worth of a case, although it is understood that the mediation process has costs associated with it.

SPECIAL ISSUES OF PERCEPTION: EMPLOYMENT DISCRIMINATION AND EXPERTS

As has probably been noticed throughout the first chapters of this volume, much of the litigation work of a consulting psychologist deals with employment litigation in various forms. Psychologists learn early in their education that psychology, the study of human behavior, is all perception and context. When the context is the legal arena, the perception of all the parties involved must be considered throughout.

Perception in Employment Discrimination Litigation

Berrey et al. (2012) observed that the perceived legitimacy of the law is really a function of the public's perception that the requisite legal processes are fair and equitable. The researchers examined situated justice to develop a contextualized analysis of the perception of fairness by litigants, employing a multimethod study of 1,788 discrimination cases that were brought to U.S. district courts. Two research-based findings were noteworthy for consulting psychologists engaged in litigation support: Neither side believes discrimination law to be fair. Instead, both plaintiffs and defendants selectively see unfairness restricted only to the processes that work to their disadvantage. Berrey et al. concluded that perceived fairness can belie structural asymmetries that serve to significantly favor employers in employment discrimination litigation.

Berrey et al.'s (2012) findings will not surprise consultants who have studied and participated in employment discrimination litigation. Support comes from social psychology, as well as the outcome statistics pertaining to the verdicts in employment discrimination litigation. Consulting psychologists can add value by counseling with their attorney-clients on either side to realistically evaluate the odds of success using a cost–benefit decision matrix. The emotional component of employment discrimination litigation is considerable and can result in poor decision making absent an objective coach with no vested interest in the outcome of the case. Frequently, settlement is the better option for both parties—although perhaps not as emotionally satisfying as a clear victory in the form of a defense or plaintiff verdict.

Perception of Expert Witnesses: Prevalence, Persuasion, and Price

Many (if not most) consulting psychologists serve as expert witnesses or recommend expert witnesses (see Chapter 2). Perceptions of such witnesses are a function of whom is asked and under what circumstances. How do jurors determine which experts to trust and believe? There are multiple dimensions to consider and evaluate, but they may not be equally relevant or predictive of competent expert testimony. The answer transcends physical appearance, attire, and how articulate the expert appears to be, although these dimensions are not entirely irrelevant.

Martire et al. (2020) addressed this question in research with jury-eligible subjects, using sample sizes in excess of 400 in each of two experiments. The researchers determined that consistency with other experts, personal ability, apparent objectivity, and trustworthiness were the most persuasive factors in determining whose testimony and expert reports to rely upon. To maximize the effectiveness of their testimony, consulting psychologists should consider these findings when engaged to coach potential witnesses.

Jurs (2016) undertook a systematic survey of judges, lawyers, jurors, and experts to determine the anticipated use and effectiveness of expert testimony in civil trials and how their professional and personal characteristics are assessed by those four participant groups. The results had considerable variance and resembled a contingency model of perceived effectiveness.

Qualities of the Expert

Expert witnesses were used in 86% of the cases, with about two thirds retained by plaintiffs. Jurs (2016) explained that from the perspective of judges and jurors as factfinders, the most salient quality of an expert is the skill to present technical information in a nontechnical way. Contrary to some prior expectations, physical appearance was the least important factor (recall Manthorpe's, 2019, very different finding regarding attractiveness of litigants as noted in Chapter 3, this volume). The experts did not disagree, but they seriously overvalued some factors, such as pleasant personality, and they undervalued other factors, such as impressive educational credentials. All groups surveyed maintained that both judges and jurors could understand expert testimony. These responses were in line with other research that demonstrated that jurors are more concerned about the actual content of the expert testimony—rather than any peripheral considerations.

Lawyers typically said that they considered qualifications and experience most paramount in their selection of experts. Impartiality was not a major consideration. Additionally, most judges who made the determination whether to permit an expert to testify relied predominantly on the expert's educational credentials and relevant experience (*Daubert v. Merrell Dow Pharmaceuticals, Inc.*, 1993). These findings are as expected and consistent with prior research. With respect to gatekeeping, most lawyers were not satisfied with judicial handling of expert qualifications, which is discussed throughout this book and most likely attributed to the *Daubert* decision and the caveat expressed by the dissent in that case (see Chapter 2).

Only 20% of lawyers thought judges did an effective job of screening experts so that only qualified experts are allowed to testify. Even fewer (15%) thought judges properly screen expert opinions to ensure they incorporated currently scientific knowledge—apparently not completely recognizing the scientific rigor standard of the *Daubert v. Merrell Dow Pharmaceuticals, Inc.* (1993) decision. Judges were most comfortable with including expert testimony, and lawyers were least comfortable. Jurors fell somewhere in between: 81% of jurors thought that being a leading expert in the field was required for an expert to be effective before a judge, yet only 22% of judges agreed.

Although these findings are sometimes contradictory regarding the most favorable qualities for an expert, the fact that must be kept in mind is that the jurors' perception is paramount. The trier of fact in most litigation will be the jury, and the jury's perception will prevail. It is a savvy forensic consulting psychologist (FCP), serving as a jury consultant, who not only understands this fact but also gets to know the expert(s) so that jurors may be chosen who will most relate to the expert(s).

The Limits of Cross-Examination

Attorneys and legal scholars generally agree that the use of cross-examination is a powerful approach in evaluating the efficacy of evidence presented through experts and an essential tool of the adversarial system of justice. The major reason is that once the proffering side opens up a topic, the opposing side has the opportunity to rebut or impeach, and that's what the jury is left with—the recency of the statement(s). There's also an old but relevant legal maxim to remember: Never ask a question you don't know the answer to. But cross-examination is not infallible.

Edmond et al. (2019) characterized the use of cross-examination as a more significant contribution to our system of law and justice than even the jury trial itself. But the researchers are not oblivious to its limitations, especially with respect to testing forensic science evidence in criminal proceedings. Even well crafted, cross-examination inquiry can be undermined by incomplete (i.e., not including known scientific research) or deceptive expert testimony that is misleading or embellished. Relying on rebuttal experts is an insufficient safeguard. Jury instructions and legal direction from a judge regarding evidence standards and burden of proof do not resolve the problem or address the gaps between scientific research and legal wisdom. Edmond et al. concluded that, with increasing reliance on forensic scientific evidence, the expectation that adversarial expert testimony and the cross-examination process will increase knowledge and improve institutional learning is not realistic.

Ethical Issues Associated With the Expert

Expert witness roles for psychologists may create an ethical conflict, or an appearance of a conflict, with their roles as mental health providers (see Chapter 2). The dual roles are not inherently conflicting, but when they occur simultaneously, involving the same client, they can be problematic and an ethical challenge. Woody (2009) addressed the multiple role issue, observing that when clinicians venture into forensic service in anticipation of professional or financial rewards, it can result in ethical quandaries. The compromise is exacerbated when practitioners lack the proper training for the multiple roles in which they elect to serve.

Attorneys inadvertently contribute to this compromise by their increasing reliance on the multiple roles of mental health practitioners. Woody (2009) noted that the objectives of traditional mental health services and expert testimony differ significantly, and thus the problems that occur when clinicians venture into forensic services should be anticipated. Attorneys and judges who are largely unfamiliar with the range of mental health specialties may inadvertently seek to press mental health practitioners into multiple roles, including potentially conflicting roles or roles for which they are not trained or qualified.

Of course, it is the ethical obligation of psychologists to point that out and not participate when they witness its occurrence (American Psychological Association [APA], 2021). Unfortunately, we cannot count on that occurring consistently, especially given the financial incentives that may be involved. Woody (2009) concluded that although not all multiple roles are ethically inappropriate, it is prudent to carefully parse them. Consulting psychologists are advised to continually review the guidelines and updates for *Ethical Principles of Psychologists and Code of Conduct* (APA, 2017) and *Specialty Guidelines for Forensic Psychology* (APA, 2013). Potential conflicts might occur among academic or behavioral science experts, fact witnesses also serving as treating therapists, expert witnesses, jury consultants and/or trial consultants, as well as professional critics of the work product of other experts.

Attorneys and judges may wish to maximize use of a mental health practitioner's knowledge and expertise for the sake of financial efficiency. But this is an inappropriate rationale for the practitioner to risk violating professional ethics. The APA Ethics Code requires psychologists to immediately attempt to resolve and manage the risk of conflict in a way to avoid or minimize harm. Psychologists are required to anticipate that the multiple roles that experts might be called upon to play could easily serve to undermine objectivity and effectiveness as psychologists in litigation or possibly expose the individual or entity with whom they have a professional relationship to possible exploitation or harm. The most appropriate course of action might be to withdraw from all but one role—or fully from the entire case.

CIVIL LIABILITY DAMAGE AWARDS

As has been repeated frequently and most likely will be repeated again, psychologists are not expected to be lawyers. Those participating in court proceedings, however, should at the very least be familiar with the terminology. *Torts* are civil wrongs against people and come in three general categories: intentional, negligent, and torts of strict liability (Legal Information Institute, *Tort*, n.d.). The tort at issue for most consultants and psychological expert witnesses is negligence; this is the basis for almost all malpractice suits (in whatever area) and products liability cases. The tort of negligence has four required elements that must be addressed by the plaintiff: Defendant must have had a duty to plaintiff, that duty was breached, the breach caused the plaintiff's damage, and that damage is measurable (or the law has ascribed a measure to it). As described in Chapters 2 and 3, tort recovery most often comes in the form of monetary damages. Intentional torts usually see the most recovery, as a certain amount of volition or intent is assumed in the act.

Negligence, however, is usually addressed in its common meaning: The defendant did not mean the harm. However, the defendant had a duty to the plaintiff not to cause harm that came as a result of the defendant's actions or omissions. As will be seen in the *Romano v. Steelcase, Inc.* (2010) example in Chapter 6, furniture manufacturers have a duty to manufacture functional furniture that will not cause harm to the consumer. The usual damage award is compensatory—the plaintiff recovers to the extent of the harm, pain and suffering, lost wages, out of pocket expenses, and so forth. However, just as most of life's experiences exist on a continuum, so does negligence. If the circumstances are egregious enough so as to be considered gross negligence (cigarette manufacturers didn't intentionally hurt anyone, but they did know or should have known the health risks of smoking), punitive damages, those damages imposed to punish and/or deter, are requested and usually awarded.

THE PSYCHOLOGY OF DAMAGE AWARDS

Greene and Bornstein (2003) noted that the job of a juror is very demanding when asked to determine damage awards due to the magnitude of evidence that may only be relevant to but a single aspect of damage determination and no others. This challenge for jurors is illustrated in that characteristics of an injury should properly serve for determining compensatory damages but not for determining punitive damages. Greene and Bornstein contrasted this with information about the wealth of a defendant, that should not be allowed to effect compensatory damage awards but that may be appropriate in determining punitive damages ("deep pockets theory")—although some may consider this practice to be unethical and not an actual legal theory. The authors expressed a healthy respect for how well jurors generally do their difficult job. They contended that more often than not, damage awards give proper weight to the elements that are supposed to be considered in their determinations—even when other credible objectives, such as (perceived) equity considerations, may be operating.

Greene and Bornstein (2003) suggested that when jurors do fall short, they tend to do so in systematic and predictable ways. Of interest to consulting psychologists is the often uneasy alliance between law and social science:

> On the one hand, social science data and conclusions are appearing ever more frequently in the courts, and policymakers are actively soliciting empirical data to guide their decision making and agenda setting. On the other hand, many social scientists feel that the courts make inadequate use of the knowledge that they have to offer, and some legal theorists feel that expert witnesses are flooding the courts with junk science. (Greene & Bornstein, 2003, p. 204)

The authors noted that a great deal of the controversy surrounds the issue of methodology, in that the empirical approaches used by social scientists incorporate good scientific methodology but may not be consistent with the principles and operation of the legal system, which continues to proceed by precedent, or previous decisions, and argument.

COGNITIVE SOCIAL PSYCHOLOGY IN EMPLOYMENT DISCRIMINATION LAW

Krieger (2004) observed that courts are prone to making use of psychological theories in cases involving discrimination but not necessarily the most recent advances in cognitive social psychology. Defense theories especially have fallen behind advances in the empirical social sciences in the context of antidiscrimination doctrine. Consulting psychologists can aid litigators by conducting the research to identify themes and stories that most resonate with the jury, and they can reinforce their case theories and have the added advantage of being easily remembered and brought into the jury room for deliberation.

This is very much akin to the constructive use of (physical) demonstrative evidence to facilitate the deliberation process. The use of compelling jury stories is understood by experienced litigators to make a significant difference in explaining and improving the understanding and retention of the most persuasive case themes. Recall the George Zimmerman defense discussed earlier in this chapter.

Settlement, Plea Bargaining, and Jury Trial Determinations

Sometimes defense attorneys become so invested in their cases (and in their clients) that they miss cues as to how egregious a jury may perceive the conduct of their client. In a wrongful termination, age discrimination, and retaliation case against an insurance carrier that relied on a large sales support operation to expand and maintain its business base, a woman with over 27 years of successful sales performance was terminated due to an illness that kept her off work and on medical leave sporadically for the greater part of the year.

The company maintained that the need for such extended leaves was disingenuous and little more than an excuse to start retirement early. The insurance carrier pressured her to return to work immediately or be terminated. The employee complained to human resources that she was being retaliated against because, when she exercised her protected right to take medical leave, there was an attempt to force her to return to work prematurely and contrary to her physician's recommendation. She did not return to work as demanded and was terminated.

The picture was complicated because the employer did have a seemingly lawful provision in the employment agreement and in its Employee Manual that limited the maximum amount of time an employee could take off work for any reason or be subject to termination, including medical leave in any one year. The employer argued this was necessary in order to maintain the continuity of business, and the policy was being uniformly enforced. I was the defense expert witness, who would have testified about the legitimacy of the employer's policy and practices and their consistency with generally accepted human resource management policy and practice. Despite the seemingly persuasive defense case, mock jurors begged to differ. Although personal feelings and ability to pay should have no bearing on jury decision making, they felt that an employee who was effective for nearly 3 decades should not be summarily dismissed because of a protracted illness, regardless of the company's contractual ability to do that. They were very angry that the company could be so heartless and uncaring to even consider terminating the employee. One mock juror commented, "Have they no decency?" It did not help the defense position that the company was shown to be enormously profitable and quite capable of operating without the plaintiff for as long as might be necessary for her complete recovery.

In 2010, I reiterated what I had observed in 2005, that

> Jurors generally try to "do the right thing" to ensure that justice (as they perceive it) is done. Jurors do not feel obligated to follow "the letter of the law" but rather take a well-meaning, common sense approach, to justice. (This is not necessarily bad.) (Finkelman, 2005, p. 46; Finkelman, 2010)

Again, and as explained in Chapter 1, angry jurors can be particularly dangerous to a defendant with respect to punitive damages. In the instant matter, the jury research was quite persuasive that this would be a risky case for the defense to litigate, despite the technical veracity of their position. The case settled shortly prior to the start of trial—the settlement provisions were not disclosed.

The present author has repeatedly made settlement recommendations to both plaintiffs and defendants (not in the same matter), when jury research demonstrated the odds were against winning at trial. Settlement recommendations in civil matters may be viewed similarly to plea bargaining in criminal matters as a compromise alternative to going to trial.

The Psychology of Litigation and Propensity for Risk

Litigation can be viewed as a form of gambling, in which the parties are calculating the odds and taking risks when they choose to file suit, engage in discovery, file motions, decline settlement offers, and elect to appeal. More than 25 years ago, Rachlinski (1996) argued that understanding litigants' proclivities for risk is essential to understanding their behavior before and during trial. Of interest to consulting psychologists serving in a litigation support capacity is the tangible possibility that, because of the difficulty of accurately predicting the probability of a favorable outcome, litigants' decision making may not be realistic or consistent with rational theories of behavior. Consulting psychologists, however, can rely in part on jury research and thus serve as the objective voices of reason and advocates for rational decision making.

Rachlinski (1996) maintained that the dominant model of litigation may be the economic model of suit and settlement. That still appears to be the case. The various components of the behavior of litigants are understandable and can be explained with respect to their economic and legal interactions, including discovery, appeal, alternate dispute resolution, and settlement.

Economics and risk-taking propensity can help clarify the gap between observed behavior and the law. The "loser-pays" system for attorney's fees in federal cases is a great example of how these interactions manifest but may not provide the complete picture. Much litigation-related behavior remains unaccounted for and is not based on the premise that litigants only make choices designed to provide them with the best economic outcome.

Modifying a purely economic model with the theories of cognitive psychology should create a richer and more accurate predictor of suit and settlement. Behavioral decision theory may come closest to providing a predictive perspective of how litigants are likely to behave. The model becomes complex because it appears that plaintiffs and defendants must make very different decisions in litigation. Settlement considerations illustrate this contrast. Plaintiffs typically choose between accepting a certain gain by settling or litigating further, knowing that the outcome is uncertain but potentially more lucrative. For defendants, the choices are either settling and accepting a certain loss or litigating further with the understanding that the outcome is uncertain and possibly more costly.

Additional factors to consider in understanding litigant decision making include a desire for justice, fairness, or just having one's day in court. Overall, it appears that behavioral decision theory still has the greatest potential to understand the behavior of litigants. But it must be considered that attorneys have significant influence on positioning the utility of various decision outcomes for their clients, thus further complicating the elegance of any predictive model.

LIE DETECTION

Finally, the topic that may or may not be explicitly addressed before, during, or even after the trial is the reason that the parties were there: to get to the truth. Addressed or not, however, it is always in the parties' thoughts. And just as psychology is about perception and context, the legal truth is about the finder of fact, usually the jury, applying those facts to the law, as instructed by the judge. In between and throughout, of course, arriving at that ultimate truth is dependent upon the truth of the evidence presented in its various forms.

The expectation that witnesses at trial are being truthful is at the core of our legal system. But the system is not naïve, and there is an understanding that this may not always be the case. The implication is that a key function of a trial is to discern truth from fabrication, whether originating in sworn testimony from the litigants or from their witnesses, fact and expert.

There is, however, an important distinction that needs to be made between the testimony of plaintiffs and defendants and the testimony of witnesses. Litigants, whether plaintiffs or defendants, are expected to be partisan. Fact and expert witnesses, from both sides, are expected to be factual and neutral, although this may not always be the case. There are frequently conflicts of interest that must be addressed; even the perception of conflicts must be anticipated and addressed prior to the other side raising the issue(s).

The standard for truthful testimony, at deposition and at trial, does not vary as a function of the status of the witness. Witnesses are sworn, under penalty of perjury, to ensure that they tell the truth at deposition and at trial. Although this is mostly a form of psychological persuasion, there are severe legal penalties associated with committing perjury. The reality, however, is that these penalties are rarely imposed, although lying or misrepresentation by witnesses and litigants under oath is probably not uncommon. A not uncommon defense to misrepresentation or lying is lack of accurate recollection (*In re Liddy*, 1973).

Except in situations that are so obvious and egregious that they are transparent to the judge (who will take appropriate corrective action), ultimately the job of lie detection falls to the jury. Juries make these judgment calls on a regular basis, when they are ostensibly comparing the testimony of partisan litigants and opposing (supposedly neutral) experts or fact witnesses. Although juries are getting more sophisticated, harder to fool, and better at seeing through fabrications by witnesses and litigants, many researchers and legal observers challenge the effectiveness of jurors as lie detectors.

Andrewartha (2008) observed that, given the seriousness and possible grave outcomes of litigation, it is expected that dishonesty is present, if not prevalent, noting that "a large body of empirical research suggests that humans, judges and jurors included, are poor at this task, with rates of accuracy predominately no greater than chance levels" (p. 88). This is concerning for all who rely on our legal system to ascertain truth and to yield fair and just verdicts at trial.

Andrewartha (2008) noted that aided lie detection techniques, such as the use of a polygraph, have yielded inconsistent results despite their claims, and the scientific basis for these devices in credibility assessment is more than questionable. Of course, one only has to refer back to the *Frye v. United States* (1923) case (see Chapter 2, this volume), when expert testimony about a polygraph test was not deemed admissible, to see that the legal support for the utilization of these devices is weak, at best. Almost a century later, courts still refuse to allow in polygraph evidence; the science wasn't generally accepted in the community in 1923, and it still hasn't met the standards of reliability of getting to the truth of the matter asserted (FRE 401, 2021).

Unfortunately, the alternative of unaided lie detection is also problematic. There are many misconceptions and little unequivocal evidence that demonstrates how liars act, who they are, and few consistent verbal and nonverbal cues that telegraph honesty or dishonesty in testimony. Individual biases and cultural stereotypes also combine to confound the accuracy of unaided lie detection.

Aided lie detection might add value to the process, but it has its own set of limitations and challenges with respect to methodology and purported success rate, especially with respect to the use of so-called lie detector devices. Andrewartha (2008) reasonably concluded that these devices, however limited, do provide greater accuracy than unaided detection techniques with reliability that is less than perfect but is greater than chance. The comparison needs to be made to the status quo of having "determinations of guilt or innocence, truth or untruth, honest or dishonest, currently rest upon 12 laypersons who bring with them a lifetime of personal and societal biases and prejudices" (Andrewartha, 2008, p. 95).

Leonetti (2017) provided an insightful analysis of the issues surrounding the use of lie detection techniques in court proceedings, noting that the concern is that of correlation, in the sense that the connection between lying and stress is too weak and inexplicable, such that it is risky to use measures of stress as predictors of deceit. Alternative approaches have been developed that do not rely on emotional response, but the author laments that they depend on implied signal detection as their validation basis. These techniques, though intriguing, have not been validated or accepted by the courts.

Because there is no truly reliable or foolproof way to determine truth from a lie, consulting psychologists, with their expertise and insight, can make a significant contribution to the process by invoking their methodological skills and scientific rigor to assist triers of fact.

SUMMARY

Most often, the FCP's job doesn't end with the end of a trial. Attorneys want to know why jurors decided the way they did. Although jurors are entitled to privacy during their deliberations, they are also permitted to discuss the case once the judgment is determined. Further, win or lose, attorneys desire to understand the FCP's insight as to why the verdict did or did not go the direction the attorney had hoped. Much of this chapter was devoted to discussion of jurors' perception, a key psychological construct, regarding defendants, plaintiffs, experts, and other parties. The chapter concluded with a discussion of lie detection, still the most controversial and elusive issue with which courts must deal.

Opportunities and Challenges for Consulting Psychologists in Litigation

The purpose of this final chapter is twofold: (a) to discuss a variety of issues that arise in the practice of forensic consulting psychologists (FCP) that might not have fit neatly into other chapters and (b) to revisit topics discussed in previous chapters that deserve further consideration. In this chapter, social media in particular, including the consulting psychologist's role, is addressed in several different ways: abuses, ethics, and juror misconduct. Ethics is further discussed from an historical perspective and regarding the expert witness. Experts, who have had a primary role in every chapter, are addressed as to those who testify and those who do not. Although mentioned in previous chapters, here two areas of jury selection and the role of the consulting psychologist are given the additional space they deserve: The voir dire process and the issue of race are always ripe areas for never-ending discussion. To conclude, the topics will be much more specific in their applicability and practicality. Consulting

https://doi.org/10.1037/0000295-006

Forensic Organizational Consulting: The Role of Psychologists in Litigation Support, by J. M. Finkelman with L. Gomberg

psychologists interact with the attorneys who hire them (and their opposing counterparts) on many levels. Finally, utilizing all that has come before, this chapter addresses the practical business of litigation contracting.

TECHNOLOGY: THE INTERNET AND SOCIAL MEDIA

A decade ago, Browning (2012) observed that approximately two thirds of adults in the United States maintain some presence on a social networking platform, and their activities are often introduced in certain court proceedings. Revelations and profiles online can be easily used to impeach witnesses, especially if the information appears to contradict their deposition or trial testimony. Investigators and corporate risk management professionals, often within a human resources (HR) department, have discovered that they can support a more compelling defense through evidence that a plaintiff is not being consistent or truthful with respect to a claim of corporate wrongdoing. It is possible, albeit more difficult, for a plaintiff to use similar trial strategies and tactics against a corporate defendant due to the lack of social media postings by corporations. Browning (2012) explained,

> Social media is here to stay, and it represents a paradigm shift in how people communicate and share information. While this digital age has given risk management and claims professionals a treasure trove of information to be mined in defending all kinds of cases, it is also proving to be a breeding ground for claims and causes of action that were unimaginable only a few years ago. (p. 30)

This is particularly relevant for job candidates who misrepresent their credentials, which can be easily verified online, or by disgruntled employees who post information on Facebook, for example, that may be inconsistent with a discrimination claim they made pertaining to sexual orientation, disability, pregnancy, or religious affiliation. Browning (2012) further cited an example in which a $10.6 million verdict in a wrongful death case in Virginia was reduced after learning that plaintiff's lawyer had directed the client to delete photos from a Facebook account that were inconsistent with claims that had been made in the lawsuit.

I testified for the plaintiffs in a case in which the pivotal issue in a negligent hiring/negligent retention lawsuit was whether a company that hired a delivery driver, who killed a customer in her home while dropping off a food order, should have known about his psychopathic propensities, which were rather transparent had they only checked his online postings. Parenthetically, to make matters worse for the defendants, simply entering the name of the delivery driver into a search engine before he was hired would have revealed an out-of-state felony conviction that was not detected in a very basic two-county, criminal background check that had been ordered by the hiring manager.

Even more relevant to this discussion would be the changes to education, socializing, and business brought about by the COVID-19 pandemic that began in the United States in 2020. As difficult as that time has proven to be, one cannot help but conjecture how much worse life would have been in all aspects of our daily living had we not had the ability to learn, meet, and conduct our business with the aid of technology.

Products Liability and Social Media

A decade-old and very small products liability case exemplifies the impact of social media in civil courts—in *Romano v. Steelcase, Inc.* (2010), Kathleen Romano's Steelcase-made desk chair collapsed under her while she was at work. Under a product liability theory, she sued Steelcase for personal injury in New York State. The defendant had access to Romano's "public" Facebook/MySpace pages but wanted access to the private pages to determine whether Romano had much more mobility after the accident than she was claiming. For some undisclosed reason, the public pages caused the suspicion that Romano was concealing a much more physically active life.

However, the federal Stored Communications Act (1986) provided that social media could not grant access unless the user gave permission. Romano refused permission. Steelcase made a pretrial motion via an Order to Show Cause, and the New York court had to weigh the applicability of the federal law against a New York State law (CPLR 3101) which provided that the defendant was entitled to all evidence available to put forth the best defense it could. Because the court held that the federal and state laws were not in direct conflict, the court granted access based on the New York law (*Romano v. Steelcase, Inc.*, 2010). No further information was ever reported about the case.

Employment Discrimination and Social Media

Employment discrimination litigation, which was discussed in more detail in Chapter 5 and earlier in this volume, may have a serendipitous outcome in facilitating needed organizational change—often through the powerful influence of social media. Deitch and Hegewisch (2013) presented an intriguing analysis, on the eve of the 50th Anniversary of the Civil Rights Act of 1964, as to how Title VII sex and race discrimination litigation settlements can provide unique opportunities to effect substantive organizational change in human resources management (HRM) policy and practice. Their study concluded that these settlements resulted in more than merely proforma compliance, instead resulting in constructive changes that fostered greater equality and inclusion.

The researchers reviewed 502 consent decrees (i.e., court orders reflecting agreement among or between the parties) in sex and race discrimination lawsuits, and they discovered that, although 48% did not trigger substantial or meaningful change, 31% required formalization of personnel decision-making remedies, while 21% required even more innovative measures. This is a very positive and perhaps largely unnoticed outcome of the litigation process that transcends merely rewarding a specific class of plaintiffs in class action lawsuits who were wronged—or only triggering short-term corrective action that was situation specific.

Although this book is in no way meant to be a treatise on the law, the reader needs to be aware that class-action lawsuits are costly, time-consuming, and rarely completely compensate the litigants for their loss. Most frequently, they are initiated by attorneys who find a similarly situated "class" of individuals who have suffered similar harm and come together to have their similar issues litigated. The attorneys need to provide notice to all potential claimants, narrow the issues through a lengthy discovery process, and file with the appropriate court to have the class "certified." If the class is certified, a named plaintiff goes through the process as would any other litigant. However, the attorney bears the costs through the settlement or award, if any. At that time, the attorneys are reimbursed and take their statutory fees from the top of the award. Whatever is left over is divided among the actual plaintiffs. Think Erin Brockovich (Clifford, 1996).

Certified class-action lawsuits filed in more liberal federal district courts and against public-sector employers resulted in the greatest likelihood of meaningful organizational change with respect to EEO-related HRM policy and practice. "Discrimination lawsuit settlements are a potential impetus for improved diversity management policies. Consent decrees are an unusually direct and potentially powerful mechanism under Title VII for employment discrimination lawsuits to mandate substantive organizational change" (Deitch & Hegewisch, 2013, p. 425).

Feaster (2016) raised yet another ethically troubling aspect of the increased use of social media to shape public opinion and awareness with respect to high-profile litigation:

> Modern politics has been marked by polarization and partisan grid-lock. With the prospects of legislative reform proving grim, interested parties seem to be more and more frequently turning to the judiciary as the best vehicle for achieving their policy ends. (p. 1013)

The concern is that this provides litigators a tempting opportunity to exploit social media to the advantage of their clients. This may well be what they are ethically obligated to do to best represent their clients' interests, in accord with the language in the American Bar Association's (ABA's; 1983) Model Rules of Professional Conduct, requiring that attorneys vehemently defend their clients to the best of their ability (see also Chapter 5, this volume). Although the Model Rules of Professional Conduct probably did not anticipate social media in its current form, the intent of the language is clear—as is the obligation to use any lawful means to protect their clients.

Consulting Psychology, Politics, and Social Media

Given the political environment of 2020 and 2021, it is easy to understand how effective social media strategy and tactics can be, but they do not necessarily serve in the best interest of justice and fairness. If consulting psychologists only know the political affiliation of a juror, they have a significant likelihood to be able to anticipate the voting inclination in a wide range of litigation matters for which political party membership accounts for much of the variance in attitudes that research demonstrates to be directly related to verdict determination. The relationship may be only correlational, rather than causal, but that doesn't make it any less valuable to litigators on both sides of a lawsuit.

Trasatti and Horevay (2013) considered the challenges related to the use of social media in the course of litigation. They recommended that trial judges immediately disclose any relationships they may have to help determine the level of engagement that is appropriate and whether the judge should even be involved with a particular case. They also took the position that

> attorneys may ethically use social media to help vet potential jurors and/or gather information from the other party's public pages, but should not "friend the other party to gain more information." Further, attorneys are advised to be aware of what they post on social media due to accidental disclosure of confidential information. (Trasatti and Horevay, 2013, p. 276)

Conflicts of interest of this nature, regarding judges, are rare but especially egregious if not disclosed to both parties. One problem that arose in the early days of social media was judges who innocently "friended" attorneys who would later appear in their courts. Attorneys and expert witnesses are vulnerable to conflicts as well, and the best protection is complete disclosure and review by a neutral source, whom in courtroom trials is typically the judge. This disclosure would be consistent with the ethical guidelines that psychologists are obligated to adhere to, as well. Ethical issues have been highlighted and considered throughout this book, but suffice it to say that the ABA and most, if not all, state bar codes of ethics have adopted specific rules regarding attorneys and their use of social media in their practices. Generally, attorneys are limited in their posting regarding their profiles, LinkedIn testimonials, blogs, and social media responses regarding the offering of services (Fairley, 2018).

Litigation Crowdfunding and Social Media

Elliott (2018) raised two significant concerns regarding the foreseeable increased use of litigation financing to pursue litigation. First, readily available funding lowers the financial threshold for a decision to initiate a lawsuit and increases the likelihood of frivolous litigation being initiated using "other people's money." By spreading the financial risk, it is probable that more risky litigation will move forward than what might otherwise be the case if it had to be funded solely by plaintiffs or their attorneys. Second, online litigation crowdfunding increases the likelihood of what Elliott called "Trial by Media," because it must inherently rely on social media in order to secure the requisite funding.

Although that process is not automatically compromising, it does raise the concern that juries may be influenced by what they discover in social media, despite the court's best effort to preclude this from occurring (see *United States v. Tsarnaev*, 2020). The increasingly pervasive (and often misleading) advertising to potential clients, typically in conjunction with offering convenient toll-free numbers for information and solicitation purposes, can be ethically troublesome. Asbestos litigation, talcum-powder litigation, ride-share accident litigation, and various medical products, as well as drug defect litigation illustrate the cause for apprehension.

There is also concern about testifying psychologists providing litigation support services at trial. The potential conflict is obvious. It is parallel to the prohibition psychologists encounter with respect to the compromises inherent in dual relationships. The safest approach is to have a focused and unambiguous role in litigation, either as an expert witness or as trial consultant. Both potential functions of consulting psychologists are explored later in this chapter.

Orozco (2016) explained the concept of "lawsourcing" as an extension of the increasingly widespread crowdsourcing model. Lawsourcing operates when a litigant initiates an open call to the online community soliciting backing to meet a legal agenda. The participants in lawsourcing may include attorneys, private individuals, government representatives, and other interested parties who need not be attorneys. Lawsourcing utilizes the cultural, social, and economic elements of crowdsourcing. Orozco commented that it can be a positive source of disruption in the legal milieu that can facilitate needed reform and improve access to services.

Although they refer to very different forms of our new technology, the internet, World Wide Web, and social media are terms that are often used interchangeably. Their origins began sometime in the 1960s or 1970s depending upon who is doing the reporting, and the fact that technological communication has become very much a part of our daily lives probably obviates the need for any distinction. Let us begin with great optimism that, by the time this volume is published, the following reference is in the past tense: During the 2020 and 2021 COVID-19 pandemic, office workers communicated with their companies via email and virtual meetings, many health care professionals "saw" patients over the internet, and children "attended" school via Zoom, GoTo Meeting, or any one of the many virtual formats that became instantly available. Families celebrated happy events by seeing each other in small squares on a computer screen, funerals were conducted virtually, and two-dimensional social, family, and school interactions became the norm.

Despite its use during the COVID-19 pandemic, the use of the internet and social media remains a topic very much debated by the courts. Attorneys, judges, and jurors are subject to discipline if the technology is misused. The State Bar of California and the ABA, for example, are prolific in issuing opinion statements on ethical technological behavior (e.g., Fairley, 2018).

Jurors and Social Media

The internet has been identified more and more frequently over the past decade as a main culprit in juror misbehavior during trials. Judges are increasingly concerned about the element of uncertainty and lack of control the unauthorized exploration of social media sites may represent. Wallace (2009) reported that the dominant reaction of the judiciary to this has been to include boilerplate language to jury instructions prohibiting such research and to remind jurors to restrict their decision making to only that evidence that is formally offered at trial. The problem, of course, is that prohibition of a juror's thought process is not directly enforceable and thus often is not effective.

Another point that should be made that might cause some of the confusion is that certain internet use is allowed. For example, the Superior Court in Orange County, California, allows and encourages future jurors waiting in the jury assembly room to bring internet devices for use during the waiting period. In fact, the brochure provided to reporting jurors and available online assures the jurors they will be provided "free wireless" access and workspaces (*Jurors/Jury Service*, n.d.). Practically speaking, and from personal experience, individuals who are assured they can carry on their workday while sitting in a waiting room are much less likely to try to beg off serving.

Because of the confusion and ambiguity, it has been suggested that trial judges be more explicit regarding the prohibited behavior and that this admonition be reinforced and emphasized prior to every trial break. To ensure that the prohibition does not appear arbitrary, prospective jurors can be taught about the issue prior to anyone being selected to serve and offered a compelling rationale to justify the prohibition. Mandatory questions can be included as part of voir dire, and jurors can be required to agree to a legal declaration acknowledging their understanding of this misconduct. Additionally, jurors can be cautioned as to the serious consequences for violation of judicial directives, which could include contempt of court charges. They can be instructed to report any instance of violation of the directive by other jurors. This would appear to be a comprehensive approach to ensure compliance that isn't otherwise occurring.

So, to summarize: The internet has enormous capacity to facilitate the ability of the public to quickly research and acquire needed information—or simply to review commentary from social networking websites. Unfortunately, that level of easy access can prove dysfunctional with respect to the misbehavior of jurors, as they search for answers about elements of a case that may intrigue or trouble them. The problem, of course, is that they are not supposed to do this. For a juror, it is essential to minimize the prejudicial effect that the introduction of extraneous material could have on the legitimacy of the verdict and the integrity of the jury process.

One need not look any further than the Federal Rules of Evidence (2021) and the admonition that even relevant evidence is not admissible if its prejudicial effect outweighs its probative value (see Chapters 1 and 3, this volume). Imagine the chaos that courts would suffer if parties had no rules about what they brought into court as fact without the other side even having an opportunity to counter the assertions.

Haralambous (2010) argued that jurors must be educated about their role and about the importance of following the judge's instructions (e.g., the *Tsarnaev* appeal years later). Beyond education, however, actual enforcement will be challenging. The present author has witnessed jurors doing exactly what they were prohibited from doing during a trial break. In the corridor outside the courtroom, two jurors were having an animated discussion about what they discovered during the court session. I was pacing the hallway, waiting to provide testimony, and it would have been completely inappropriate and not permissible to have said anything at the time—other than mentioning it, after testifying, to the attorneys who retained me (I did tell them, and they elected to do nothing).

Another common error on the part of jurors (and students and the general public) is to get information from attorney blogs. A quick search of the internet on almost any legal topic will result in a myriad of attorney blogs. These are not always obvious as advertisements, but they are and are most often written to sound authoritative—some even cite cases and statutes (L. Gomberg, personal communication, July 27, 2020).

To control juror misuse of social media, an increasing number of states and federal districts have adopted jury instructions with varying degrees of specificity and effectiveness in response to expanding cases involving allegations of juror misconduct involving social media. Jurors are typically instructed not to conduct their own research or investigation about the case from any source other than the courtroom. In this age of technology, we all know people who seemingly use their smartphones as appendages to their thought processes; this is especially common among young adults. It is not unusual to sit in a restaurant, for example, and see people checking, texting, or even talking on their phones instead of conversing with tablemates. Very few seem to be able to resist the temptation to check email or look up the "real answer" to a question that has come up during a social interaction.

If this is acceptable behavior during social interaction, jurors may continue that same behavior without knowing that what they are doing is wrong. For example, I have heard attorneys refer to obvious distortions in the mass media with the likely intent of tempting jurors to check out the exaggerated information. However, as juror usage of social media has become a recognized problem in the courts, California (and probably other states) enacted a bill in 2016 that allows a judge to fine a juror up to $1,500 for knowingly violating a court order (California Code of Civil Procedure § 177.6, 2016). Apparently, the enactment of this law was in direct response to the observed increase of juror use of social media (Temme, 2019). Consulting psychologists, especially jury consultants, need to be concerned with the ethical and legal implications of juror conduct, if they are involved in the litigation process and monitor juror behavior accordingly.

Aaronson and Patterson (2013) proposed two innovative model jury instructions designed to reduce juror confusion, enable jurors to better understand the importance of the restrictions on their out-of-court research activities, and direct their attention to the serious consequences of violating the court's instructions. They proposed that clear language should be employed pertaining to the use of social media and that specific examples regarding prohibited social media activities be provided, along with the logic behind any restrictions that are imposed, as well as the legal consequences for violating them. Of course, such admonitions have to be based on fact and law to carry any weight, and courts are very busy places with very busy jurists, who are much more interested in resolving legal issues than investigating them. In fact, in reversing and remanding the *Tsarnaev* case sentencing verdict and judgment, in 2020, the U.S. First Circuit Court of Appeals (2020) stated that they were able to review and do so at least partially because they had the "luxury of time that district judges rarely have" (p. 5).

Lest anyone think the impact of social media in legal verdicts is being overemphasized, that same decision should quell the notion (see Chapter 4). In 2013, Dzhokhar Tsarnaev and his older brother set off two bombs at the Boston Marathon and killed or injured over 200 people and killed an MIT campus police officer during their escape. The older brother was also killed, but Dzhokhar was captured, tried, convicted, and sentenced to death. His lawyers have been appealing ever since.

On August 1, 2020, the *Los Angeles Times* (and dozens of other news outlets) reported that the court had overturned the death sentence because "the [district court] judge ... did not adequately screen jurors for potential biases" (p. A12). Although this is not exactly accurate reporting, the basis of the decision generally was judicial error; specifically, the three-judge panel stated, among other reasons, that the trial judge had been under a duty to inquire about the potential jurors' knowledge about the case. At least partially because two of the jurors had posted on social media their own biased opinions the day before the trial began, the death sentence was overturned. Although social media and juror misconduct were definitely factors in the decision, it must also be kept in mind these were not the sole reasons for the remand and reversal. The decision cited 16 different areas upon which the appeal was based. The appeals court reversed three of the convictions on weapons charges and remanded the sentencing phase back to a trial court. This, of course, means a new jury could again sentence the defendant to death or to life without the possibility of parole. The court was very clear and very concerned that this defendant would not under any circumstances leave prison (*United States v. Tsarnaev*, 2020).[1]

The Internet and the Jury Trials: An Equivocal Relationship

These issues, with respect to misuse of the internet, in no way minimize the very positive influence technology can have in helping juries to understand the complexity of a case. Software programs have been developed to preclude internet classroom cheating by students at schools and universities, and they will likely be applicable to court settings as well. This can be

---

[1]As of October 2021, the United States appealed the 2020 decision to the U.S. Supreme Court. As of February 2022, the Court hasn't rendered a decision.

done without compromising the ability of the internet to positively impact proceedings at trial and enable better understanding of case issues that might be pivotal to jurors in rendering a just verdict.

Hoffmeister and Watts (2018) seemed skeptical about the net value of the internet and social media on the trial by jury process. Although acknowledging positive effects, such as enhancing the ability to inform and communicate quickly with prospective jurors and allowing attorneys' to more easily investigate the background and perspective of jurors as part of the voir dire process, they determined that such technological innovations create more threats than actual opportunities for the ongoing viability of the jury system.

Hoffmeister and Watts (2018) explained that although jury trials require the jurors to be unbiased, the pervasive influence of the internet and social media have served to make it less probable that unbiased jurors will be available for empanelment. Once selected, jurors will likely be curious to attain unauthorized outside intelligence, which will serve to precipitate prohibited conversations with both jurors and nonjurors, inside and outside the courtroom. Collectively, these compromises can undermine the fundamental integrity of the jury process.

Hoffmeister and Watts (2018) advocated for additional research to better understand the scope of the problem and possible solutions. They noted that the research can be conducted electronically or via mail questionnaires to courtroom personnel, judges, attorneys, and jurors. The questionnaires need to tap the evolving ways jurors are using the internet and incorporate specific questions about juror misconduct. The questionnaires should also examine whether ongoing reforms are effective. A research environment needs to be created that is conducive to juror truth-telling. For that reason, rather than surveying jurors in the courthouse, they need to be contacted posttrial, when and where they feel safe and secure in being candid and acknowledging misconduct, if that was the case. This recommendation, however, proves to be quite interesting; the researchers suggested the use of the very medium that they're criticizing in order to gather factual information.

As a professor of graduate psychology students, and chair and member of an institutional review board, Linda Gomberg finds that the subject of internet research is frequently raised. Although the method certainly garners significantly more responses than actual mail or personal survey or interviews, it does not provide any check on the veracity of the responses or the responders. Students can now employ companies to collect, sort, and input their data. Just as the internet has provided multiple methods and services for obtaining information quickly and thoroughly on almost any topic, it has also provided an outlet for anonymous falsehoods and misrepresentation.

Online Jury Selection

HRM professionals have learned that an expedited approach to getting information about job candidates is to simply enter their names into a search engine and see what emerges. In fact, the present author recently testified for plaintiffs in a negligence in hiring/negligence in retention lawsuit, explaining that the hiring of an employee who committed manslaughter could have been easily avoided if the employer just bothered to research the applicant's name, which would have instantly revealed devastating information about his past criminal activities. Similarly, litigators are able to do essentially the same thing as a way to quickly access a wide array of information about prospective jurors prior to their selection.

Neal et al. (2013) reflected on the utility of readily accessible social networking sites and other online sources to discover a myriad of useful information about potential jurors. Attorneys are obligated and prone to eliminate biased jurors and perhaps even to attempt to select jurors who are favorably disposed toward their clients. The authors noted that privacy concerns issues for jurors had not yet been established in case law. They conducted two investigations regarding the potential invasion of privacy and discovered useful information for more than one third of jurors researched. Remarkably, sophisticated searches were not necessary, in that 94% of the data were accessible using very basic internet searches. Accordingly, the researchers advocated for the most parsimonious solution in unobtrusively acquiring this intelligence through rudimentary searches.

Maybe even more to the point is that historically, when privacy and the public's right to know have conflicted with each other, the public's right to know almost invariably wins. The former is part of tort law and a psychological construct; the latter is often construed as a First Amendment issue in that the right to know is akin to freedom of speech and expression (Gomberg, 2012). Although this may be the reason that no case law on the subject could be found in 2013 and does not seem to exist 8 years later, somehow, the U.S. Supreme Court has apparently forgotten that the Bill of Rights was the document that created "penumbras," or zones of privacy that are implicit in every one of the rights enumerated (see *Griswold v. Connecticut*, 1965). Of course, in today's zeitgeist, it is often forgotten that, in 1791, the first 10 Amendments to the new U.S. Constitution (1789) were written to protect individuals from unwarranted government intrusion and not intrusion by one another (Gomberg, 2012).

Neal et al. (2013) also solicited responses from lawyers, students, and consultants about ensuing personal privacy and ethical issues that might emerge associated with the use of the internet to acquire this type of information. Not surprising to most consulting psychologists, all groups surveyed had concerns about the privacy rights of all parties to litigation and the implications for the entire legal process.

ETHICAL ISSUES FOR FCPs

The skill sets of FCPs within the mental health profession have not escaped the notice of litigators representing both sides of disputes. Although not all psychologists actually practice as mental health clinicians, they are all educated about mental health. The relevance for FCP is a function of the significant number of state-licensed psychologists who are also forensic consulting psychology–trained consultants and HR professionals. Kaufman (2011) reflected on the ethical challenges these dual roles may present when taken out of their court-appointed roles as neutral evaluators or mediators and invited into potentially partisan roles, as part of litigation teams by attorneys representing opposing sides in a conflict:

> Forensic Mental Health Professionals must conform to the ethical requirements of their discipline, while still conducting themselves in accord the obligations and demands of litigation. Forensic psychologists have been engaged in mental health related legal cases for over a century. (p. 5)

Kaufman (2011) observed that litigation consultants have been engaged in trial preparation and related research for a long time, although participating at trial for only about 60 years. During that time, they crafted ethical guidelines and professional practice requirements to direct their professional conduct. Testifying psychologists and FCPs can gain an understanding and learn a great deal from the legal profession and its respective ethics code (see Chapter 5).

Among the ethical concerns providing litigation support services may raise for consulting psychologists is the troubling question of which side can best afford to utilize their services. That answer is usually quite straightforward (i.e., the defense), but the ethical considerations are more convoluted. With respect to psychologists serving as expert witnesses in employment-related matters, there is typically greater equity as I've experienced in over 60 cases of providing expert testimony.

It is rare for one side to utilize an expert witness without the other side following suit (so to speak). But on occasion, I served as an expert witness for plaintiffs in a trial for which defendants did not feel that expert testimony was necessary or appropriate. Similarly, on occasion, I served as an expert witness for defendants in a trial for which plaintiffs did not feel that expert testimony was necessary or appropriate.

Typically, in these circumstances, the opposing side tries to persuade the court to exclude the opposing expert—or at least limit the scope of such testimony. The failure of either side to accomplish that tactical objective usually does not bode well for the party objecting to the testimony. It is a high threshold for a court to agree to entirely exclude an opposing expert, which might also constitute grounds for appeal if the side unable to utilize its expert doesn't prevail at trial. But it is far more common and included in the FRE to have the scope of expert testimony limited to only areas of testimony that the court determines would assist the trier of fact (typically the jury) render a fair and just verdict.

This is often the subject of contentious negotiation between the attorneys for both parties and the presiding judge, which occurs outside of the presence of a jury. Arguments in this regard typically occur before the jury is even seated but can sometimes occur during a break in the trial in the privacy of the judge's chambers. Legal briefs may be ordered from both sides to assist the judge in making a ruling.

Strier (1999) raised challenging ethical issues for FCPs who are engaged in trial consulting. Because of its increasing prevalence in major litigation, it is appropriate to question the cost effectiveness, as well as the fairness of trial consulting. Strier asked whether it might also impair the impartiality of the jury and whether it is ethical if only one side is able to use the services of trial consultants. Less obvious is the question of whether this type of consulting may serve to undermine the public's perception of jury trial fairness and legitimacy. Since jury trials are in many ways the essence of our legal system, this is a significant concern.

There is also concern about testifying psychologists providing litigation support services at trial. The potential conflict is obvious. It is parallel to the prohibition psychologists encounter with respect to the compromises inherent in dual relationships. The safest approach is to have a focused and unambiguous role in litigation—either as an expert witness or as a trial consultant.

JURY SCIENCE (ONE MORE TIME)

Gruppie and Perez (2006) observed a growing trend toward empirically based jury selection and trial consulting; that trend has become more pervasive since they wrote about it. Even 15 years ago, many legal observers were arguing that, in large cases, failure to use trial consultants is almost a type of malpractice. The alternative was speculation and intuition into jurors' personal biases and attitudes. Gruppie and Perez noted that the result of empirical jury selection may be hard to measure accurately, but the consensus of trial attorneys is that jury consultants and mock trials are associated with successful results.

Advocates for scientific jury and trial consulting acknowledge that the process is geared toward anticipating and shaping trial outcomes. Gruppie and Perez (2006) quoted practitioners who maintained that they exceeded 90% accuracy in anticipating the verdict of a trial even prior to the presentation of evidence. Although some may challenge the exact percentage, my direct experience is quite consistent with that representation.

The focus of leading litigation consulting firms is on strategic persuasion, sometimes characterized as the essence of litigation. Gruppie and Perez (2006) examined the boundary between the power of jury science and the ethical issues it presents to FCPs. According to the authors, some psychologists and related professionals represent jury science to be essentially "high-tech jury tampering." The ethical challenge, as proposed by some with differing political views, is focused on a fear that if trial verdicts can be altered by having consultants scientifically select juries, the entire jury system of justice would be tainted as unfair and inequitable and might not be able to sustain itself over time.

Gruppie and Perez (2006) bristled at the implication that jurors are not able to render verdicts that are limited to the evidence to which they are exposed during trial. In addition, if the public learns that jury consultants used science to somehow alter a trial verdict, it could diminish the perceived integrity of that verdict. Admittedly, there may be merit to that concern. The problem, as Gruppie and Perez anticipated, is that juror independence is a basic core of our system of jurisprudence, that cannot be compromised without grave risk. The opposing position, in support of scientific jury selection, argues that the science preserves judicial autonomy by ensuring that potential underlying prejudice is detected and is not allowed to insidiously change the outcome of a trial.

The authors concluded by noting that regardless of any potential ethical concerns, it is a litigant's absolute right, not to mention a lawyer's duty, to use all legal and ethical means available to litigate their case (Gruppie & Perez, 2006). This compelling interpretation would thus preclude any restrictions being imposed on hiring jury consultants. That position appears to have prevailed over time and in all probability will continue.

What may be the most interesting part of this whole discussion is that as much as jury science may be criticized, jury selection methodology is frequently criticized because it lacks rigor and standardized assessments. This is contrary to the training of most consulting psychologists and leaves ample opportunity for adding value to the voir dire process. Lecci et al. (2004) advocated for incorporating standardized, proven methods to detect and address opportunities for pretrial juror bias and thus allow for greater efficiency in the voir dire process. The authors advanced the need to scientifically evaluate the contribution of trial consultants in order to determine whether it adds enough value to justify the cost.

The Juror Bias Scale (Kassin & Wrightsman, 1983) is an example of a classic measure that was developed to assess pretrial bias, typically in criminal trials. Scale items assess juror bias on issues of probability of commission and reasonable doubt, as well as juror confidence and cynicism in the criminal justice system. The Civil Trial Bias Scale (Wrightsman & Heili, 1992) is a standardized questionnaire that can be used in civil trials. In summary, the use of standardized assessments helps consulting psychologists and trial consultants quantify bias in prospective jurors and generate more accurate verdict predictions.

FINAL WORD(S) ON RACE AND JURY SELECTION

Psychologists recognize that race has an influence on many aspects of society, and that includes the legal system (as has been discussed throughout this volume). McGuffee et al. (2007) studied the perception jurors had about the fairness of the jury system and the role of race in juror selection. The results were rather complex and ambiguous—and sometimes inconsistent with prior research findings. A few outcomes were noteworthy: Jurors who served or were selected for service were more likely to perceive the system as racially neutral and fair. Overall, actual experience with the jury system was likely to result in a more positive impression of its efficacy and lack of racial bias, possibly because they saw the process in action in real time.

Older jurors were also more likely to view the system as fair and less likely to believe that juror composition needed to be representative of the general population with respect to race. However, age was not related to whether jurors viewed the process as racially neutral. Higher income jurors generally did not perceive the system as unbiased as those who were less well off, but this finding did not hold at the multivariate level. Gender was, somewhat surprisingly, not correlated with any perception of bias or fairness.

McGuffee et al. (2007) argued that the findings regarding income were counterintuitive. The logic was that higher income jurors were more likely to be isolated from any adverse socioeconomic, class-based aspects of the justice system and would be more comfortable in assuming it was fair and unbiased. However, that was not what the research revealed. Instead, higher socioeconomic class jurors were more likely to perceive racial bias operating, although education level was not measured or controlled in the research.

Perhaps the most interesting finding for consulting psychologists is that, despite the general assumption that racially diverse juries reduce the probability of a racially biased outcome, respondents' views about the need for juries to be racially diverse was not predictive of their views as to the overall fairness of the system with respect to racial bias.

Ethical Issues for Forensic and Consulting Psychologists as Expert Witnesses

Swanepoel (2010) advocated addressing and curtailing instances of unethical and unprofessional conduct by testifying psychologists and thus reducing resulting malpractice suits. Psychology is a regulated profession with the well-developed, frequently revised, and earlier mentioned *Ethical Principles of Psychologists and Code of Conduct* (APA Ethics Code; APA, 2017). The Ethics Code consists of Standards and Principles that cover just about every aspect of the profession. The Standards are enforceable rules for professional conduct subject to discipline and malpractice suits, whereas the Principles are aspirational, goals that the ideal psychologist aspires to attain.

Further, in light of the unique requirements for forensic psychologists in their role(s) in the legal arena, *Specialty Guidelines for Forensic Psy-chology* (Specialty Guidelines; APA, 2013) have been developed. Of course, guidelines are aspirational with no legal effect, but they do serve to define and refine the role of the psychologist whose practice revolves around a legal purpose. Expert testimony by psychologists has become an essential part of the legal process, highlighting the need for ethical behavior and defensible decision making. In the service of those objectives, consulting psychologists serving as expert witnesses are advised to take steps to ensure compliance and protect themselves against allegations of professional misconduct.

Although there should probably be no need to remind psychologists of their ethical and legal responsibilities, specific recommendations include understanding and complying with the APA Ethics Code and staying informed about relevant legislation, which is constantly changing, especially with respect to patient and client confidentiality, privacy, and informed consent. This means that psychologists whose practices include going to court need to be familiar with local court rules and relevant laws (as stated in earlier chapters), the Health Insurance Portability and Accountability Act, as well as the Ethics Code and the Specialty Guidelines, all with their most recent amendments or updates. Psychologists need to self-regulate and understand how to identify and address any ethical challenges and compliance issues that may emerge—and consult with trusted colleagues when uncertain as to what needs to be done to ensure sound ethical practice.

TRIAL CONSULTANTS VERSUS NONTESTIFYING EXPERTS

There are two kinds of experts, but they share a common expertise. One testifies; the other doesn't. The underlying knowledge and competencies may be the identical, but the skill sets needed to be effective differ significantly. Gould et al. (2011) observed that although the roles of trial consultant and testifying expert witness share many functions, they are not interchangeable. The field of forensic psychology has evolved, and there is a developing consensus that keeping these roles separate and distinct is beneficial for the forensic practitioner, attorneys, the courts, and the litigants.

Although they may seem repetitious, Gould et al. (2011) offered three important suggestions to maintain the distinction and thus the integrity of the process:

1. Attorneys should not ask experts to serve in the dual role of consultant to the legal team and testifying expert witness. Experts are also

best advised to avoid engaging in dual roles—and the ethical compromises that might be inherent in such service. In fact, Guideline 11.02 of the Specialty Guidelines might be referring to just that situation, when saying in part "Forensic practitioners are encouraged to explain the relationship between their expert opinions and the legal issues and facts of the case at hand" (p.16). Although the Guideline ends at that point, it seems to imply that the practitioner also needs to distinguish those roles.

2. Attorneys should have a clear, written agreement with the expert regarding exactly which one of the two possible roles will be required by the legal team.

3. The designated "client" engaging the expert should be the legal team rather than the litigant, in order to protect the confidentiality of the expert's work product. In fact, Appendix B of the Specialty Guidelines defines "client" as, among others "the attorney . . . who has retained and has a contractual relationship with the forensic practitioner" (p. 9).

Again, the distinction may seem petty and innocuous—until problems or conflicts arise. The potential ethical compromises and consequences are quite substantive. Thus, the logic of full disclosure and transparency at the beginning of the relationship, to avoid misunderstandings, before any harm is done, is of paramount importance. Consulting experts may or may not become testifying experts and are not typically disclosed, unless they provide sworn testimony.

Caudill (2018) observed that in Australia which uses a similar legal system to the United States, there is an interesting colloquial distinction made between "a clean and a dirty expert" (p. 338). In Great Britain and Australia, so-called clean experts have a duty only to the court and are bound, as such, by a specific code of conduct. In contrast, so-called dirty experts are considered part of the legal team of a litigant, described as advocacy-oriented—and their objectivity is suspect.

Caudill (2018) commented, rather scornfully, that in the United States there are seemingly no ethical concerns about a consulting expert converting to a testifying expert, a scenario that would trigger red flags in Australia because of the potential conflict inherent in such a transition.

A critical ethical question that consulting psychologists may wish to ponder is whether an attorney in the United States should be permitted to keep confidential and not disclose to opposing counsel all conversations with a consulting expert or to a testifying expert who is later engaged. Of course, the ethical standards for psychologists do not vary, regardless of whether they are serving as consulting or testifying experts. Best practice may still be having two separate experts, if litigation budgets permit.

THE ETHICS AND LEGALITY OF JURY TRIAL CONSULTING

Over the years, ethical criticism has been offered as to the appropriateness of one side potentially being able to manipulate a jury outcome by utilizing expensive outside resources for jury research, trial strategy, and general trial consultation.

Historical Perspective

Jury trials existed well before the U.S. Constitution was written over 200 years ago. Many perceive such trials as the truest form of justice. The deduction is that jury trials, with all their faults (see Chapter 2), are probably as good as a justice system can be, although fine-tuning and enhancement are always possible.

In 1996, Martinez provided an excellent historical perspective and overview of the questions and controversy associated with the use of jury consultants. Our jury system is first memorialized in Article III, Section 2, of the U.S. Constitution. It requires that all criminal cases (other than impeachment) be tried by an impartial jury. The Sixth Amendment grants the right to an impartial jury in all criminal cases, and the Fourteenth Amendment, among other rights, guarantees that the states will also provide due process and equal protection under the law (as does the Fifth Amendment, which provides the same protections as respects the federal government). The intent was to be certain the citizenry was protected from arbitrary federal and state government decisions.

Although Martinez (1996) wrote 25 years ago, the issue of considering whether it is feasible to use jury consultants and still not infringe upon the rights of others or creating an imbalance in our adversarial system of justice by encumbering poor citizens and advantaging the rich is still current and relevant. These issues are ongoing and raise questions that consulting psychologists, among others, should be considering in their professional practice, although they may not be positioned to address the concerns directly. Legal ethicists have a great deal to review and upon which to reflect. Among the many other questions, they have been asked to consider the question of socioeconomic status of the parties. This consideration immediately suggests a 2-decade-old question: Would O. J. Simpson have been acquitted in his murder trial if he had not had the celebrity and financial resources to assemble his legal "dream team?" The answer is (for many reasons beyond the scope of this book): Most probably not. The integrity of the justice system is at stake in deliberating and coming to a resolution of these questions.

Beyond the ethics of using consultants to scrutinize potential jurors and thus potentially alter the outcome of a trial, one needs to consider whether *not* using a jury consultant might constitute a violation of the attorneys' obligation to use every possible legal means to zealously advocate for their clients. That's an insightful question that is expressly stated as an ethical obligation in the Preamble to the American Bar Association's Model Rules of Professional Conduct (2020).

Ethical Concerns of Employing Jury Consultants to Assist in the Jury Selection Process

In my experience, most attorneys and judges favor the use of jury questionnaires to enhance the effectiveness of courtroom trials. Semerdjian and Mulligan (2019) commented that a main reason to use jury consultants is to detect hidden bias in potential jurors, which can then guide attorneys as to when it is necessary to expend their limited peremptory challenges, if a case cannot be made to exclude a juror for cause. The authors referred to jury selection as the make-it-or-break-it phase of a trial. That perspective is consistent with research cited elsewhere in this book.

PRACTICAL (AND USEFUL) CONSIDERATIONS

Although lawyers are sometimes perceived as overly compensated merce-naries who enjoy the good life at the expense of their clients and the rest of us, that is not the reality. Although many lawyers are well compensated, others struggle to earn a living and work hard to survive. Even highly compensated senior partners at major law firms must work hard to grow and maintain their practice, while at the same time supervising asso-ciates and junior partners. Why wouldn't these privileged professionals be satisfied and happy with their lives and jobs? Many are, but the picture is mixed.

In my experience, having interacted over the years as an expert witness with hundreds of attorneys, a few consistent themes emerged. Successful attorneys work extremely hard as they prepare cases and defenses for trial. At the same time, they are always focused on developing and maintaining their client base and keeping them satisfied and loyal. The fear of a loss in court weighs heavily on them. Their clients are often characterized as dif-ficult to please and sometimes problematic.

When attorneys are sufficiently comfortable to speak candidly, two themes emerge that adversely intrude on their well-being and quality of life: law firm politics and gender discrimination, the later point most fre-quently raised by female partners. It would probably be naïve to assume that law firms would somehow be immune to these issues. They aren't. In that sense, law firms are organizations that mirror the issues afflicting most organizations, some legal, some ethical, and some structural. Effec-tive leadership can help, but they can't ameliorate these concerns.

Consulting psychologists can be involved at multiple levels. Their psychological training allows them to provide personal support, as appro-priate, while their organizational training permits them to address some of the structural issues that may underlie these concerns. The present author has been surprised at the level of personal angst expressed by some plaintiff and defense clients for whom he has repeatedly served as an expert witness.

I've prepped with attorneys the night before trial and tried to help them deal with anxiety and uncertainty that typically would not emerge.

The reader should be cautioned that these experiences are based almost exclusively with litigators and thus not necessarily generalizable to all attorneys.

Davis-Laack and Krill (2018) referenced a 2016 study by Krill et al. surveying almost 13,000 practicing attorneys that found much higher than average drinking, depression, stress, and anxiety. The authors noted that for some attorneys, the problem started in law school with high rates of depression, anxiety, and binge drinking. The solution probably needs to revert to the law school experience as well.

Consulting psychologists may interact with their lawyer-clients at multiple levels. The present author has been asked to counsel and coach lawyers, often in conjunction with a primary engagement as a testifying expert witness, if doing so didn't create role conflicts or other ethical issues. As such, it is useful to understand the general satisfaction mindset of attorneys with whom consulting psychologists deal in whichever of the many capacities that have been discussed in this book. Chambers (2014) reviewed more than two dozen statistically based studies reporting that most lawyers claim to be satisfied with their job.

But the author contended that these studies convey an "overly rosy" impression of lawyers' attitudes: many lawyers putting themselves above midpoints on job satisfaction are only slightly more positive than negative about their careers—and ambivalent about their work (Chambers, 2014, p. 313). There was also concern that surveys conducted at any one point in time do not include those who have since left and gone elsewhere. Finally, bias may be introduced because the least satisfied lawyers in the population sampled might have lower response rates.

Chambers (2014) summarized the ambivalent research: One body of literature reports that attorneys are miserable, and another report indicates that, in overwhelming numbers, attorneys are satisfied with their jobs. "Taken together, a revised view would alter not at all one highly important finding of the surveys—that only a small proportion of attorneys hold negative views overall about their jobs or careers" (Chambers, 2014, p. 330). In fact, anecdotal literature about attorneys indicating that population to be extremely unhappy may be inaccurate and not representative of attorneys in general. Chambers maintained that, despite the negative literature regarding attorney job satisfaction and ambivalence about many aspects of their jobs, "nothing in the survey literature, properly viewed, should be seen as inconsistent" (p. 330).

I beg to differ. It is not realistic to homogenize attorney satisfaction when the reality is that there is a dichotomy among practicing attorneys in this regard. Among the hundreds of attorneys with whom I consulted, over more than 3 decades, the overwhelming majority were very satisfied—although very overworked. The few who were not satisfied did not appear to be as successful as those who were. This may be the most parsimonious way to account for the variance that some researchers have observed. Not surprisingly, successful attorneys may be more content with their careers than their less successful counterparts. The differential success variable alone may account for much of the experimental variance that others have observed. Admittedly, I have had the good fortune to work with predominantly highly successful plaintiff and defense attorneys, thus my sample of attorneys, though large, may not be representative of the profession.

Up until his death in 2020, one Southern California retired attorney, who had been a member of the State Bar (happily, he claimed) for 59 years, created a new career calling himself the "Happy Lawyer Coach" (J. Bame, dec., personal communications, 2010–2020). His business continued to thrive as he spoke all over the country attracting attorneys who were either not happy or not successful or both in their practices.

Regardless of the perspective and interpretation of attorney job satisfaction, it seems apparent that consulting psychologists can do more to aid their attorney-clients than simply provide traditional litigation support services. Their psychological training can add significant incremental value to the relationship.

In 2019, Spier and Prescott introduced the intriguing option of contingent contracting through which the opposing parties in litigation can negotiate and attempt to mitigate risk prior to trial. They note that litigation contracting has the double downside of reducing the rates of settlement, as well as raising the already considerable expenses associated with engaging in litigation. The resulting contracts provide a form of insurance and an approach to risk management that is somewhat akin to organizations that fund the cost of litigation, in the anticipation and hope for a favorable outcome at trial, which would be shared with them. It is likely that the frequency of contingent contracting will increase as the frequency and costs of litigation escalate. However, although contingency fees are not considered unethical in the legal profession, they most definitely are frowned upon for consulting/forensic psychologists. Specialty Guideline 5.02 (2013) explains the problem: "Because of the threat to impartiality presented by the acceptance of contingent fees and associated legal prohibitions, forensic practitioners strive to avoid providing professional services on the basis of contingent fees" (p. 12). This, then, is the best illustration of one of the earlier truisms stated in this volume: Consulting psychologists are paid for their time, their expertise, their neutrality, and their experience.

SUMMARY

This final chapter introduced, reviewed, and elaborated on many of the themes that are part of the FCP's responsibilities. Specifically, the chapter delved into the FCP's work with attorneys, their code of ethics, and the impact of technology. Social media in particular plays a large role in the day-to-day operation of today's law and psychology. The FCP must be well versed in the APA *Ethical Principles of Psychologists and Code of Conduct*, as well as the *Specialty Guidelines for Forensic Psychology*. A major takeaway for FCPs, not only from this chapter but from the entire volume, is the ability to interact positively and effectively with attorneys, whether on behalf of their plaintiff- or defendant-clients.

Finally, the goal throughout this volume has been to guide the emerging FCP to be a positive and effective resource from the initiation of a case until its conclusion and to clarify that role. The goal is not to create "wannabe" attorneys but rather to provide a working familiarity with the complexities of the legal system within which they will need to operate. No more need be said.

References

Aaronson, D. E., & Patterson, S. M. (2013, Winter). Modernizing jury instructions in the age of social media. *Criminal Justice*, *27*(4), 26–35. https://digitalcommons.wcl.american.edu/cgi/viewcontent.cgi?article=1233&context=facsch_lawrev

Afanador, V. A. (2018, August). Diversity in jury selection and the evolving limitations on peremptory challenges. *New Jersey Lawyer*, 57–60. https://www.litedepalma.com/77A1CC/assets/files/Documents/Afanador.pdf

Age Discrimination in Employment Act, 29 U.S.C. § 623 (1967). https://www.law.cornell.edu/uscode/text/29/623

Allen v. Hannaford, 138 Wash. 423, 244 P. 700 (1926).

American Bar Association. Model Rules of Professional Conduct. (1983). *Preamble.*

American Bar Association. Model Rules of Professional Conduct. (2020). *Preamble.* https://www.americanbar.org/groups/professional_responsibility/publications/model_rules_of_professional_conduct/model_rules_of_professional_conduct_preamble_scope/

American Psychological Association. (2013). Specialty guidelines for forensic psychology. *American Psychologist*, *68*(1), 7–19. https://doi.org/10.1037/a0029889

American Psychological Association. (2017). *Ethical principles of psychologists and code of conduct* (2002, amended effective June 1, 2010, and January 1, 2017). https://www.apa.org/ethics/code/ethics-code-2017.pdf

American Psychological Association. (2021, February). *APA-approved standards and guidelines.* https://www.apa.org/about/policy/approved-guidelines#

American Society of Trial Consultants. (n.d.). *Mission and history.* ASTC. https://www.astcweb.org/history_mission_statement

Americans With Disabilities Act of 1990, 42 U.S.C. § 12101 (1990). https://www.ada.gov/pubs/adastatute08.htm

Anderson, R. T. (2020). On the basis of identity: Redefining "sex" in civil rights law and faulty accounts of "discrimination." *Harvard Journal of Law & Public Policy, 43*(2), 387–423. https://www.harvard-jlpp.com/wp-content/uploads/sites/21/2020/03/JLPP-Full-Vol-43-Issue-2.pdf

Andrewartha, D. (2008). Lie detection in litigation: Science or prejudice? *Psychiatry, Psychology and Law, 15*(1), 88–104. https://doi.org/10.1080/13218710701873940

Andrews, C. K. (2009). *Shadow juries: Benefits and limitations.* Practicing Law Institute. http://www.pli.edu/emktg/all_star/shadowjur_benefits02.doc

Aron, R., & Rosner, J. L. (1998). *How to prepare witnesses for trial* (2nd ed.). West Publishing.

Barefoot v. Estelle, 463 U.S. 880 (1983).

Barry, A. K. (1991). Narrative style and witness testimony. *Journal of Narrative and Life History, 1*(4), 281–293. https://doi.org/10.1075/jnlh.1.4.02sty

Barthe, E. P., Leone, M. C., & Lateano, T. A. (2013). Commercializing success: The impact of popular media on the career decisions and perceptual accuracy of criminal justice students. *Teaching in Higher Education, 18*(1), 13–26. https://doi.org/10.1080/13562517.2012.694099

Bates, K. G. (Host). (2013, July 14). *National reaction to the Zimmerman verdict: "What next?"* [Audio podcast]. NPR. https://www.npr.org/sections/codeswitch/2013/07/14/202131045/National-Reaction-To-The-Zimmerman-Verdict-What-Next

Batson v. Kentucky, 476 U.S. 79 (1986).

Baumann, F., & Friehe, T. (2012). Emotions in litigation contests. *Economics of Governance, 13*(3), 195–215. https://doi.org/10.1007/s10101-012-0110-1

Berrey, E., Hoffman, S. G., & Nielsen, L. B. (2012). Situated justice: A contextual analysis of fairness and inequality in employment discrimination litigation. *Law & Society Review, 46*(1), 1–36. https://doi.org/10.1111/j.1540-5893.2012.00471.x

Bersoff, D. N. (2013, June). APA's amicus briefs: Informing public policy through the courts. *Monitor on Psychology, 44*(6), 5.

Blumstein, P. W., Carssow, K. G., Hall, J., Hawkins, B., Hoffman, R., Ishem, E., Maurer, C. P., Spens, D., Taylor, J., & Zimmerman, D. L. (1974). The honoring of accounts. *American Sociological Review, 39*(4), 551–566. https://doi.org/10.2307/2094421

Boccaccini, M. T. (2002). What do we really know about witness preparation? *Behavioral Sciences & the Law, 20*(1–2), 161–189. https://doi.org/10.1002/bsl.472

Bornstein, B. H., Golding, J. M., Neuschatz, J., Kimbrough, C., Reed, K., Magyarics, C., & Luecht, K. (2017). Mock juror sampling issues in jury simulation research: A meta-analysis. *Law and Human Behavior, 41*(1), 13–28. https://doi.org/10.1037/lhb0000223

Bornstein, B. H., & Greene, E. (2011). Jury decision making: Implications for and from psychology. *Current Directions in Psychological Science, 20*(1), 63–67. https://doi.org/10.1177/0963721410397282

Bostock v. Clayton County, 140 S. Ct. 1731 (2020).

Brief for American Psychiatric Association, as Amicus Curiae, Supporting Appellant in Jenkins v. United States, 307 F.2d 637 (D.D.C. 1962).

Bright, D. A., & Goodman-Delahunty, J. (2011). Mock juror decision making in a civil negligence trial: The impact of gruesome evidence, injury severity, and information processing route. *Psychiatry, Psychology and Law, 18*(3), 439–459. https://doi.org/10.1080/13218719.2010.492095

Brodsky, S. L., & Pivovarova, E. (2016). The credibility of witnesses. In C. Willis-Esqueda & B. H. Bornstein (Eds.), *The witness stand and Lawrence S. Wrightsman, Jr.* (pp. 41–52). Springer. https://doi.org/10.1007/978-1-4939-2077-8_4

Browning, J. G. (2012, October 8). "Like" it or not: How social media can lead to litigation. *Risk Management Magazine.* https://www.rmmagazine.com/articles/article/2012/10/08/-Like-It-or-Not-How-Social-Media-Can-Lead-to-Litigation-

Burgoon, J. K., Birk, T., & Pfau, M. (1990). Nonverbal behaviors, persuasion, and credibility. *Human Communication Research, 17*(1), 140–169. https://doi.org/10.1111/j.1468-2958.1990.tb00229.x

California Code of Civil Procedure, *Sanctions: Jurors,* § 177.6 (2016).

Campo, A. (2015, August 3). Feedback groups: Useful low-cost tool for trial consultants and their clients. *The Jury Expert, 27*(3). https://www.thejuryexpert.com/2015/08/feedback-groups-a-useful-low-cost-tool-for-trial-consultants-and-their-clients/

Carlson, S. (2017). E-jury consultant: Powered by IBM Watson, Voltaire gives lawyers real-time predictions on how potential jurors might vote. *ABA Journal, 103*(11), 32–34.

Caudill, D. S. (2018). "Dirty" experts: Ethical challenges concerning, and a comparative perspective on, the use of consulting experts. *St. Mary's Journal on*

Legal Malpractice and Ethics, 8(2), 338–373. https://commons.stmarytx.edu/cgi/viewcontent.cgi?article=1008&context=lmej

Chambers, D. L. (2014). Overstating the satisfaction of lawyers. *Law & Social Inquiry*, 39(2), 313–333. https://doi.org/10.1111/lsi.12041

Chorn, J. A., & Kovera, M. B. (2019). Variations in reliability and validity do not influence judge, attorney, and mock juror decisions about psychological expert evidence. *Law and Human Behavior*, 43(6), 542–557. https://doi.org/10.1037/lhb0000345

Civil Rights Act of 1964, Pub. L. No. 88–352, 78 Stat. 241 (1964).

Clark, J., Boccaccini, M. T., Caillouet, B., & Chaplin, W. F. (2007). Five factor model personality traits, jury selection, and case outcomes in criminal and civil cases. *Criminal Justice and Behavior*, 34(5), 641–660. https://doi.org/10.1177/0093854806297555

Clifford, F. (1996, July 3). Utility to pay $333 million to settle suit. *Los Angeles Times*. https://www.latimes.com/archives/la-xpm-1996-07-03-mn-20787-story.html

Cohen, L. J. (1997). Meeting the challenge of the "junk science" defense in domestic violence litigation. *Psychotherapy: Theory, Research, & Practice*, 34(4), 397–409. https://doi.org/10.1037/h0087740

Connolly, P. R. (1982). Persuasion in the closing argument: The defendant's approach. In G. W. Holmes (Ed.), *Opening statements and closing arguments: Speeches and demonstrations from a decade of advocacy institutes* (pp. 159–164). The Institute of Continuing Legal Education.

Cooper, J., Bennett, E. A., & Sukel, H. L. (1996). Complex scientific testimony: How do jurors make decisions? *Law and Human Behavior*, 20(4), 379–394. https://doi.org/10.1007/BF01498976

Cooper, J., & Neuhaus, I. M. (2000). The "Hired Gun" effect: Assessing the effect of pay, frequency of testifying, and credentials on the perception of expert testimony. *Law and Human Behavior*, 24(2), 149–171. https://doi.org/10.1023/A:1005476618435

Cornell, R. M., Warne, R. C., & Eining, M. M. (2009). The use of remedial tactics in negligence litigation. *Contemporary Accounting Research*, 26(3), 767–787. https://doi.org/10.1506/car.26.3.5

Coughlan, S. M. (2019). The (im)partial jury: A trial consultant's role in the venire process. *Brooklyn Law Review*, 84(2), 671–702. https://brooklynworks.brooklaw.edu/blr/vol84/iss2/9/

Cover, A. P. (2017). Hybrid jury strikes. *Harvard Civil Rights-Civil Liberties Law Review*, 52, 357–396. https://www.njcourts.gov/courts/assets/supreme/judicialconference/CoverHybridJury.pdf?c=2Kc

Crocker, C. B., & Kovera, M. B. (2010). The effects of rehabilitative voir dire on juror bias and decision making. *Law and Human Behavior*, 34(3), 212–226. https://doi.org/10.1007/s10979-009-9193-9

Cutler, B. L. (1990). Introduction: The status of scientific jury selection in psychology and law. *Forensic Reports, 3*(3), 227–232. https://psycnet.apa.org/record/1991-01076-001

Cutler, B. L., Penrod, S. D., & Dexter, H. R. (1990). Juror sensitivity to eyewitness identification evidence. *Law and Human Behavior, 14*(2), 185–191. https://doi.org/10.1007/BF01062972

Daftary-Kapur, T., Dumas, R., & Penrod, S. D. (2010). Jury decision-making biases and methods to counter them. *Legal and Criminological Psychology, 15*(1), 133–154. https://doi.org/10.1348/135532509X465624

Daly, M. (2015). Foster v. Chatman: Clarifying the Batson test for discriminatory peremptory strikes. *Duke Journal of Constitutional Law & Public Policy Sidebar, 11*, 148–162. https://scholarship.law.duke.edu/cgi/viewcontent.cgi?referer=&httpsredir=1&article=1131&context=djclpp_sidebar

Daubert v. Merrell Dow Pharmaceuticals, Inc., 509 U.S. 579 (1993).

Davis-Laack, P., & Krill, P. (2018, February). How and why to bring the lawyer well-being "movement" to your law firm. *National Association for Law Placement, PD Quarterly*, 5–9. https://stressandresilience.com/wp-content/uploads/2019/07/How-and-Why-to-Bring-the-Lawyer-Well-Being-PDL-PK-2019.pdf

DeAngelis, T. (2019, December). Informing the courts with the best research. *Monitor on Psychology, 50*(11), 48. https://www.apa.org/monitor/2019/12/cover-courts#

Deitch, C., & Hegewisch, A. (2013). Title VII sex and race discrimination litigation settlements as opportunities for organizational change. *Journal of Business and Psychology, 28*(4), 425–438. https://doi.org/10.1007/s10869-013-9294-9

DeMatteo, D., Fishel, S., & Tansey, A. (2019). Expert evidence: The (unfulfilled) promise of Daubert. *Psychological Science in the Public Interest, 20*(3), 129–134. https://doi.org/10.1177/1529100619894336

D'Esposito, J. M. (2016). The role of nonverbal persuasion in juror decision-making and the need to regulate the trial consulting industry. *Notre Dame Journal of Law, Ethics & Public Policy, 30*(1), 143–174. https://heinonline.org/HOL/LandingPage?handle=hein.journals/ndlep30&div=9&id=&page=

Des Rosiers, N., Feldthusen, B., & Hankivsky, O. A. R. (1998). Legal compensation for sexual violence: Therapeutic consequences and consequences for the judicial system. *Psychology, Public Policy, and Law, 4*(1–2), 433–451. https://doi.org/10.1037/1076-8971.4.1-2.433

Draft Memo Re Batson-Wheeler Motions. (n.d.). Superior Court of the State of California. https://www.aclunc.org/sites/default/files/2019.09.11%20Marin%20Batson%20Training%20Materials.pdf

Drogin, E. Y. (2007). The forensic psychologist as consultant: Examples from a jurisprudent science perspective. *The Journal of Psychiatry & Law, 35*(3), 245–260. https://doi.org/10.1177/009318530703500302

Edmond, G., Cunliffe, E., Martire, K., & San Roque, M. (2019). Forensic science evidence and the limits of cross-examination. *Melbourne University Law Review, 42*(3), 858–919.

Edwards, H. T., & Mnookin, J. L. (2016, September 20). A wake-up call on the junk science infesting our courtrooms. *The Washington Post.* https://www.washingtonpost.com/opinions/a-wake-up-call-on-the-junk-science-infesting-our-courtrooms/2016/09/19/85b6eb22-7e90-11e6-8d13-d7c704ef9fd9_story.html

Eisenberg, J. R. (2005). *Law, psychology & death penalty litigation.* Professional Resource Press.

Ekman, P. (1989). Why lies fail and what behaviors betray a lie. In J. C. Yuille (Ed.), *NATO Science: Series D. Behavioral and social sciences* (Vol. 47, pp. 71–81). Springer. https://doi.org/10.1007/978-94-015-7856-1_4

Ekman, P., & Friesen, W. V. (1969). The repertoire of nonverbal behavior: Categories, origins, usage, and coding. *Semiotica, 1*(1), 49–98. https://doi.org/10.1515/semi.1969.1.1.49

Elliott, M. (2018). Trial by social media: The rise of litigation crowdfunding. *University of Cincinnati Law Review, 84*(2), 529–552.

Fairley, S. (2018, August 8). 4 Tips for attorneys navigating the social media ethics minefield. *The National Law Review.* https://www.natlawreview.com/article/4-tips-attorneys-navigating-social-media-ethics-minefield

Farr, J. L., & Tippins, N. T. (Eds.). (2017). *Handbook of employee selection.* Taylor & Francis.

Feaster, M. J., Jr. (2016). Blogging and the political case: The practice and ethics of using social media to shape public opinion in anticipation of high-profile litigation. *The Georgetown Journal of Legal Ethics, 29,* 1013.

Federal Rules of Evidence. (2021).

Federal Rules of Evidence 401. (2021). https://www-law-cornell-edu.libproxy1.usc.edu/rules/fre/rule_401

Federal Rules of Evidence 402. (2021). https://www-law-cornell-edu.libproxy1.usc.edu/rules/fre/rule_402

Federal Rules of Evidence 403. (2021). https://www-law-cornell-edu.libproxy1.usc.edu/rules/fre/rule_403

Federal Rules of Evidence 606. (2021). https://www.law.cornell.edu/rules/fre/rule_606

Federal Rules of Evidence 702. (2021). https://www.law.cornell.edu/rules/fre/rule_702

Federal Rules of Evidence 703. (2021). https://www-law-cornell-edu.libproxy1.usc.edu/rules/fre/rule_703

Federal Rules of Evidence 801. (2021). https://www.law.cornell.edu/rules/fre/rule_801

Federal Rules of Evidence 803. (2021). https://www.law.cornell.edu/rules/fre/rule_803

Finkelman, J. M. (2005). Juror perception of employment litigation. *The Psychologist-Manager Journal, 8*(1), 45–54. https://doi.org/10.1207/s15503461tpmj0801_5

Finkelman, J. M. (2010). Litigation consulting: Expanding beyond jury selection to trial strategy and tactics. *Consulting Psychology Journal, 62*, 12–20.

Fitzgerald, L. F., Buchanan, N. T., Collinsworth, L. L., Magley, V. J., & Ramos, A. M. (1999). Junk logic: The abuse defense in sexual harassment litigation. *Psychology, Public Policy, and Law, 5*(3), 730–759. https://doi.org/10.1037/1076-8971.5.3.730

Forsterlee, L., Kent, L., & Horowitz, I. A. (2005). The cognitive effects of jury aids on decision-making in complex civil litigation. *Applied Cognitive Psychology, 19*(7), 867–884. https://doi.org/10.1002/acp.1124

Foster v. Chatman, 136 Sup. Ct. 1737 (2016).

Fox, P., Wingrove, T., & Pfeifer, C. (2011). A comparison of students' and jury panelists' decision-making in split recovery cases. *Behavioral Sciences & the Law, 29*(3), 358–375. https://doi.org/10.1002/bsl.968

Frick, R. W. (1985). Communicating emotion: The role of prosodic features. *Psychological Bulletin, 97*(3), 412–429. https://doi.org/10.1037/0033-2909.97.3.412

Frye v. United States, 293 F. 1013 (D.C. Circuit 1923).

Garcia, R. (2017, January 26). A real data scientist reviews Bull's "trial science." *Vijilent.* https://www.vijilent.com/real-data-scientist-reviews-tv-trial-science/

Garner, B. A. (Ed.). (2019). *Black's law dictionary* (11th ed.). Thomson West.

Giannelli, P. C. (1993). "Junk science": The criminal cases. *The Journal of Criminal Law & Criminology, 84*(1), 105–128. https://doi.org/10.2307/1143887

Gies, L. (2005). Law as popular culture: Cross-disciplinary encounters. *Continuum: Journal of Media & Culture Studies, 19*(2), 165–180. https://doi.org/10.1080/10304310500084376

Goldstein, A. M. (2005). Law, psychology & death penalty litigation [Review of the book *Law, psychology & death penalty litigation*, by J. R. Eisenberg]. *The Journal of Psychiatry & Law, 33*(1), 123–126. https://doi.org/10.1177/009318530503300109

Gomberg, L. (2018). *Forensic psychology 101.* Springer. https://doi.org/10.1891/9780826140753

Gomberg, L. J. (2012). *The case for privacy: A history of privacy in the United States as seen through a psychological lens and defined by case law and the impact of social media (whatever happened to "it's none of your business"?)* (Publication No. 3493470) [Doctoral dissertation, Fielding Graduate University]. ProQuest Dissertations and Theses Global.

Gould, J., Martindale, D., Tippins, T., & Wittmann, J. (2011). Testifying experts and non-testifying trial consultants: Appreciating the differences. *Journal of Child Custody: Applying Research to Parenting and Assessment Practice and Policies, 8*(1–2), 32–46. https://doi.org/10.1080/15379418.2010.547442

Greathouse, S. M., Sothmann, F. C., Levett, L. M., & Kovera, M. B. (2011). The potentially biasing effects of voir dire in juvenile waiver cases. *Law and Human Behavior, 35*(6), 427–439. https://doi.org/10.1007/s10979-010-9247-z

Greenbaum, T. L. (1998). Litigation focus groups. In T. L. Greenbaum (Ed.), *The handbook for focus group research* (2nd ed., pp. 154–160). SAGE Publications. https://doi.org/10.4135/9781412986151.n10

Greene, E. (2003). Psychology in civil litigation: An overview and introduction to the special issue. *Law and Human Behavior, 27*(1), 1–4. https://doi.org/10.1023/A:1021608710316

Greene, E., & Bornstein, B. H. (2003). *Determining damages: The psychology of jury awards.* American Psychological Association. https://doi.org/10.1037/10464-010

Griffith, J. D., Hart, C. L., Kessler, J., & Goodling, M. M. (2007). Trial consultants: Perceptions of eligible jurors. *Consulting Psychology Journal: Practice and Research, 59*(2), 148–153. https://doi.org/10.1037/1065-9293.59.2.148

Griswold v. Connecticut, 381 U.S. 479 (1965).

Gruppie, G. R., & Perez, G., III. (2006). Ethical issues in the use of trial consultants. *FDCC Quarterly, 56*, 267–278.

Gunnell, J. J., & Ceci, S. J. (2010). When emotionality trumps reason: A study of individual processing style and juror bias. *Behavioral Sciences & the Law, 28*(6), 850–877. https://doi.org/10.1002/bsl.939

Guthrie, C. (2000). Framing frivolous litigation: A psychological theory. *The University of Chicago Law Review, 67*(1), 163–216. https://doi.org/10.2307/1600328

Haby, J. A., & Brank, E. M. (2013, April). The role of anchoring in plea bargains. *Monitor on Psychology, 44*(4), 30. https://www.apa.org/monitor/2013/04/jn

Hamilton, M. C., & Zephyrhawke, K. (2015, November). Revealing juror bias without biasing your juror: Experimental evidence for best practice survey and voir dire questions. *The Jury Expert: The Art and Science of Litigation Advocacy, 27*(4), 1–7.

Haralambous, N. (2010). Educating jurors: Technology, the internet and the jury system. *Information & Communications Technology Law, 19*(3), 255–266. https://doi.org/10.1080/13600834.2010.533454

Helm, R. K., Hans, V. P., Reyna, V. F., & Reed, K. (2020). Numeracy in the jury box: Numerical ability, meaningful anchors, and damage award decision making. *Applied Cognitive Psychology, 34*(2), 434–448. https://doi.org/10.1002/acp.3629

Herndon, W. W., & Karl, J. J. (1978). Demonstration: Preparation of a witness to testify. *Antitrust Law Journal, 47*(1), 123–140. https://www.jstor.org/stable/40839938

Hilbert, J. (2019). The disappointing history of science in the courtroom: Frye, Daubert, and the ongoing crisis of "junk science" in criminal trials. *Oklahoma Law Review, 71,* 759–821. https://digitalcommons.law.ou.edu/olr/vol71/iss3/3

Hoffmeister, T., & Watts, A. C. (2018). Social media, the internet, and trial by jury. *Annual Review of Law and Social Science, 14*(1), 259–270. https://doi.org/10.1146/annurev-lawsocsci-101317-031221

Hollier, R. (2017, March). Physical attractiveness bias in the legal system. *The Law Project.* https://static1.squarespace.com/static/5817bb2746c3c4a605334446/t/58cb53ebe4fcb52ea33b8b8a/1489720308340/Attractiveness+Bias+in+the+Legal+System+by+Rod+Hollier.pdf

Horowitz, I. A., Kerr, N. L., Park, E. S., & Gockel, C. (2006). Chaos in the courtroom reconsidered: Emotional bias and juror nullification. *Law and Human Behavior, 30*(2), 163–181. https://doi.org/10.1007/s10979-006-9028-x

Hunt, J. S. (2015). Race, ethnicity, and culture in jury decision making. *Annual Review of Law and Social Science, 11*(1), 269–288. https://doi.org/10.1146/annurev-lawsocsci-120814-121723

Huntley, J. E., & Costanzo, M. (2003). Sexual harassment stories: Testing a story-mediated model of juror decision-making in civil litigation. *Law and Human Behavior, 27*(1), 29–51. https://doi.org/10.1023/A:1021674811225

Hutchins v. Municipal Court, 132 Cal. Rptr. 158, 61 Cal. App. 3d. 77 (Cal. Ct. App. 1976).

Jacobson, J., Dobbs-Marsh, J., Liberman, V., & Minson, J. A. (2011). Predicting civil jury verdicts: How attorneys use (and misuse) a second opinion. *Journal of Empirical Legal Studies, 8*(S1), 99–119. https://doi.org/10.1111/j.1740-1461.2011.01229.x

Jenkins v. United States, 307 F. 2d 637 (D.C. Cir. 1962).

Jones, A. M., & Kovera, M. B. (2015). A demonstrative helps opposing expert testimony sensitize jurors to the validity of scientific evidence. *Journal of Forensic Psychology Practice, 15*(5), 401–422. https://doi.org/10.1080/15228932.2015.1090225

Joy, P. A., & McMunigal, K. C. (2016). Racial discrimination and jury selection. *Criminal Justice, 31,* 43–45.

Jurors/Jury service. (n.d.). The Superior Court of California: County of Orange. https://www.occourts.org/directory/jury-services/

Jurs, A. (2016). Expert prevalence, persuasion, and price: What trial participants really think about experts. *Indiana Law Journal*, *91*, 353–391.

Kafadar, K. (2017). The critical role of statistics in demonstrating the reliability of expert evidence. *Fordham Law Review*, *86*, 1617.

Kassin, S. M., & Wrightsman, L. S. (1983). The construction and validation of a juror bias scale. *Journal of Research in Personality*, *17*(4), 423–442. https://doi.org/10.1016/0092-6566(83)90070-3

Kaufman, R. L. (2011). Forensic mental health consulting in family law: Where have we come from? Where are we going? *Journal of Child Custody: Research, Issues, and Practices*, *8*(1), 5–31. https://doi.org/10.1080/15379418.2010.547441

Kelley, J. (2013, July 12). Document: Instructions for George Zimmerman jury. *The Atlanta Journal-Constitution*.

Kotla v. Regents of University of California, 115 Cal. App. 4th 283, 8 Cal. Rptr. 898 (Cal. Ct. App. 2004).

Krieger, L. H. (2004). The intuitive psychologist behind the bench: Models of gender bias in social psychology and employment discrimination law. *Journal of Social Issues*, *60*(4), 835–848. https://doi.org/10.1111/j.0022-4537.2004.00389.x

Krill, P. R., Johnson, R., & Albert, L. (2016). The prevalence of substance use and other mental health concerns among American attorneys. *Journal of Addiction Medicine*, *10*(1), 46–52. https://doi.org/10.1097/ADM.0000000000000182

Kumho Tire Co. v. Carmichael, 526 U.S. 137 (1999).

Lambert, W. (1994, February 4). Lawyers and clients. *The Wall Street Journal*, B7.

Langbein, J. (2012). The disappearance of civil trial in the United States. *The Yale Law Journal*, *122*, 522–572.

Leathers, D. G. (1997). *Successful nonverbal communication* (3rd ed.). Allyn and Bacon.

Lecci, L., & Myers, B. (2008). Individual differences in attitudes relevant to juror decision making: Development and validation of the Pretrial Juror Attitude Questionnaire (PJAQ). *Journal of Applied Social Psychology*, *38*(8), 2010–2038. https://doi.org/10.1111/j.1559-1816.2008.00378.x

Lecci, L., Snowden, J., & Morris, D. (2004). Using social science research to inform and evaluate the contributions of trial consultants in the voir dire. *Journal of Forensic Psychology Practice*, *4*(2), 67–78. https://doi.org/10.1300/J158v04n02_04

Lee, C. (2015). A new approach to voir dire on racial bias. *UC Irvine Law Review*, *5*(4), 843–872. https://doi.org/10.2139/ssrn.2729432

Lee, S. (2014). Plea bargaining: On the selection of jury trials. *Economic Theory*, *57*(1), 59–88. https://doi.org/10.1007/s00199-014-0801-7

Legal Information Institute. (n.d.). *Damages*. https://www.law.cornell.edu/wex/damages

Legal Information Institute. (n.d.). *Deposition*. https://www.law.cornell.edu/wex/deposition

Legal Information Institute. (n.d.). *Tort*. https://www-law-cornell-edu.libproxy1.usc.edu/wex/tort

Leonetti, C. (2017). Abracadabra, hocus pocus, same song, different chorus: The newest iteration of the "science" of lie detection. *Richmond Journal of Law & Technology, 24*(1), 1–36. https://jolt.richmond.edu/volume24_issue1_leonetti/

Leshem, E. A. (2019). Jury selection as election: A new framework for peremptory strikes. *Yale Law Review, 128*, 2356–2411.

Levett, L. M., & Kovera, M. B. (2008). The effectiveness of opposing expert witnesses for educating jurors about unreliable expert evidence. *Law and Human Behavior, 32*(4), 363–374. https://doi.org/10.1007/s10979-007-9113-9

In Re Liddy, 506 F.2d 1293 (D.C. Cir. 1973) (grand jury proceedings).

Lieberman, J. D. (2011). The utility of scientific jury selection: Still murky after 30 years. *Current Directions in Psychological Science, 20*(1), 48–52. https://doi.org/10.1177/0963721410396628

Lieberman, J. D., Krauss, D. A., Heen, M., & Sakiyama, M. (2016). The good, the bad, and the ugly: Professional perceptions of jury decision-making research practices. *Behavioral Sciences & the Law, 34*(4), 495–514. https://doi.org/10.1002/bsl.2246

Lieberman, J. D., & Sales, B. D. (2007). *Scientific jury selection*. American Psychological Association. https://doi.org/10.1037/11498-000

Lisko, K. O. (1992). *Juror perceptions of witness credibility as a function of linguistic and nonverbal power* (Publication No. 9313134) [Doctoral dissertation, University of Kansas]. ProQuest Dissertations and Theses Global.

Lundrigan, S., Dhami, M. K., & Mueller-Johnson, K. (2016). Predicting verdicts using pre-trial attitudes and standard of proof. *Legal and Criminological Psychology, 21*(1), 95–110. https://doi.org/10.1111/lcrp.12043

Luongo, M. (2018). Throwing out junk science: How a new rule of evidence could protect a criminal defendant's right to confront forensic scientists. *Journal of Law and Policy, 27*, 221–256.

Manthorpe, S. (2019). Physical attractiveness in the courts. *California Legal Studies Journal*, 61–70.

Martinez, P. L. (1996). *The constitutional, legal, and ethical concerns of employing jury consultants to assist in the jury selection process* [Unpublished master's thesis]. Southwest Texas State University.

Martire, K. A., Edmond, G., & Navarro, D. (2020). Exploring juror evaluations of expert opinions using the expert persuasion expectancy framework. *Legal and Criminological Psychology, 25*(2), 90–110. https://doi.org/10.1111/lcrp.12165

Mathie, J. (2016, December 20). A second opinion can be helpful . . . or not. *Wisconsin Law Journal*. https://www.mediate.com/JMathie/docs/A%20Second%20Opinion%20Can%20Be%20Helpful,%20Or%20Not%20-%20Wis%20L%20Journ%2012-21-2016.pdf

Matlon, R. J. (1988). *Communication in the legal process*. Holt, Rinehart & Winston Inc.

McCarthy Wilcox, A., & NicDaeid, N. (2018). Jurors' perceptions of forensic science expert witnesses: Experience, qualifications, testimony style and credibility. *Forensic Science International, 291*, 100–108. https://doi.org/10.1016/j.forsciint.2018.07.030

McConahay, J. B., Mullin, C. J., & Frederick, J. (1977). The uses of social science in trials with political and racial overtones: The trial of Joan Little. *Law and Contemporary Problems, 41*(1), 205–229. https://doi.org/10.2307/1191235

McCormick, C. T. (1955). Some highlights of the uniform evidence rules. *Texas Law Review, 33*(5), 559–573.

McCormick on Evidence §13 (1955).

McGraw, P., Attanasio, P., & Garcia, R. (Executive Producers). (2016–Present). *Bull* [TV series]. Amblin Television; CBS.

McGuffee, K., Garland, T. S., & Eigenberg, H. (2007). Is jury selection fair? Perceptions of race and the jury selection process. *Criminal Justice Studies, 20*(4), 445–468. https://doi.org/10.1080/14786010701758245

Mehrabian, A. (1971). *Silent messages*. Wadsworth.

Miller, K. (2019, February 5). *Shadow juries are priceless, but do not expect TV land biometrics*. Courtroom Logic.

Molski v. Arby's Huntington Beach, 359 F. Supp. 2d 938 (C.D. Cal. 2005).

Montz, C. L. (2001). Why lawyers continue to cross the line in closing argument: An examination of federal and state cases. *Ohio Northern Law Review, 28*, 67–131. https://heinonline.org/HOL/LandingPage?handle=hein.journals/onulr28&div=8&id=&page=

Moore, A. (1989). Trial by schema: Cognitive filters in the courtroom. *UCLA Law Review, 37*, 273–340.

Morgan, S., & Palk, G. (2013). Pragmatism and precision: Psychology in the service of civil litigation. *Australian Psychologist, 48*(1), 41–46. https://doi.org/10.1111/j.1742-9544.2012.00075.x

Mulvaney, M. D., & Litter, J. (2015). The importance of voir dire: Essential techniques for choosing finders of fact. *The American Journal of Trial Advocacy, 39*(2), 313–338.

Nagle, J. E., Brodsky, S. L., & Weeter, K. (2014). Gender, smiling, and witness credibility in actual trials. *Behavioral Sciences & the Law, 32*(2), 195–206. https://doi.org/10.1002/bsl.2112

Neal, T. M. S. (2009). Expert witness preparation: What does the literature tell us? *Journal of Expertise, 21*, 44–52.

Neal, T. M. S., Cramer, R. J., Ziemke, M. H., & Brodsky, S. L. (2013). Online searches for jury selection. *Criminal Law Bulletin, 49*, 305–318.

Neal, T. M. S., Slobogin, C., Saks, M. J., Faigman, D. L., & Geisinger, K. F. (2019). Psychological assessments in legal contexts: Are courts keeping "junk science" out of the courtroom? *Psychological Science in the Public Interest, 20*(3), 135–164. https://doi.org/10.1177/1529100619888860

Nemire, K. (2011). Cognitive human factors in litigation. *Ergonomics in Design, 19*(1), 16–20. https://doi.org/10.1177/1064804611400988

Nielsen, J. C. (2005). Human resources management comes of age in the courtroom: California formally enshrines the importance of human resources expert testimony for employment litigation. *The Psychologist Manager Journal, 8*(2), 157–164. https://doi.org/10.1207/s15503461tpmj0802_6

Nielsen, L. B., Nelson, R. L., & Lancaster, R. (2010). Individual justice or collective legal mobilization? Employment discrimination litigation in the post civil rights United States. *Journal of Empirical Legal Studies, 7*(2), 175–201. https://doi.org/10.1111/j.1740-1461.2010.01175.x

Norton, M. I., Sommers, S. R., & Brauner, S. (2007). Bias in jury selection: Justifying prohibited peremptory challenges. *Journal of Behavioral Decision Making, 20*(5), 467–479. https://doi.org/10.1002/bdm.571

Norton, S. D., & Gustafson, D. P. (1982). Industrial/organizational psychology as applied to human resources management. *Professional Psychology, 13*(6), 904–917. https://doi.org/10.1037/0735-7028.13.6.904

Nuñez, N., McCrea, S. M., & Culhane, S. E. (2011). Jury decision making research: Are researchers focusing on the mouse and not the elephant in the room? *Behavioral Sciences & the Law, 29*(3), 439–451. https://doi.org/10.1002/bsl.967

O'Barr, W. M. (1982). *Linguistic evidence: Language, power, and strategy in the courtroom.* Academic Press.

Obergefell v. Hodges, 574 U.S. 1118 (2015).

Ogloff, J. R. P. (1999). Law and human behavior: Reflecting back and looking forward. *Law and Human Behavior, 23*(1), 1–7. https://doi.org/10.1023/A:1022328305624

Orozco, D. (2016). The use of legal crowdsourcing ("lawsourcing") to achieve legal, regulatory, and policy objective. *American Business Law Journal, 53*(1), 145–192. https://doi.org/10.1111/ablj.12074

Parrott, C. T., Neal, T. M., Wilson, J. K., & Brodsky, S. L. (2015). Differences in expert witness knowledge: Do mock jurors notice and does it matter? *The Journal of the American Academy of Psychiatry and the Law, 43*(1), 69–81. https://pubmed.ncbi.nlm.nih.gov/25770282/

Pena-Rodriguez v. Colorado, 137 S. Ct. 855 (2017).

Penrod, S., & Cutler, B. (1995). Witness confidence and witness accuracy: Assessing their forensic relation. *Psychology, Public Policy, and Law, 1*(4), 817–845. https://doi.org/10.1037/1076-8971.1.4.817

People v. Wheeler, 22 Cal. 3d 258, 148 Cal. Rptr. 890, 583 P.2d 748 (1978).

Peter-Hagene, L. C., & Bottoms, B. L. (2017). Attitudes, anger, and nullification instructions influence jurors' verdicts in euthanasia cases. *Psychology, Crime & Law, 23*(10), 983–1009. https://doi.org/10.1080/1068316X.2017.1351967

Peter-Hagene, L. C., & Ratliff, C. L. (2021). When jurors' moral judgments result in jury nullification: Moral outrage at the law as a mediator of euthanasia attitudes on verdicts. *Psychiatry, Psychology and Law, 28*(1), 27–49. https://doi.org/10.1080/13218719.2020.1751741

Prescott, D. E. (2015). Forensic experts and family courts: Science or privilege-by-license. *Journal of the American Academy of Matrimonial Lawyers, 28,* 521–552.

Pyszczynski, T. A., & Wrightsman, L. S. (1981). The effects of opening statements on mock jurors' verdicts in a simulated criminal trial. *Journal of Applied Social Psychology, 11*(4), 301–313. https://doi.org/10.1111/j.1559-1816.1981.tb00826.x

Queen v. M'Naghten, 8 Eng. Rep. 718 (1843).

Rachlinski, J. J. (1996). Gains, losses, and the psychology of litigation. *Southern California Law Review, 70,* 113–185.

Richards, J. (2017). A call to arms to regulate arbitration consulting. *Dispute Resolution Journal, 72*(4), 41–48.

Rieke, R. D., & Stutman, R. K. (1990). *Communication in legal advocacy.* University of South Carolina Press.

Robbennolt, J. K., & Studebaker, C. A. (2003). News media reporting on civil litigation and its influence on civil justice decision making. *Law and Human Behavior, 27*(1), 5–27. https://doi.org/10.1023/A:1021622827154

Robertson, C., Yokum, D., & Robertson, C. T. (2012). The effects of blinded experts on juror verdicts. *Journal of Empirical Legal Studies, 9*(4), 765–794. https://doi.org/10.1111/j.1740-1461.2012.01273.x

Romano v. Steelcase, Inc., 30 Misc. 3d 426, 907 N.Y.S.2d 650 (2010).

Roper v. Simmons, 543 U.S. 551 (2005).

Rose, M., Murphy, B., & Smith, S. (2006). Juror questions during trial: A window into juror thinking. *Vanderbilt Law Review, 59,* 1927–1972.

Ryan, J. W., Jr. (2010). The disappearing civil jury trial. *Defense Counsel Journal, 77,* 425–426.

Ryan, M. E., & Svaldi, D. (1993). Women in the courtroom: Increasing credibility through nonverbal behavior change. *Trial Diplomacy Journal, 16,* 253–259.

Sanctions: Jurors, CA CCP § 177.6 (2016).

Schlenker, B. R. (1980). *Impression management: The self-concept, social identity, and interpersonal relations.* Brooks/Cole.

Schmitt, N. (2013). Research in *Consulting Psychology Journal: Practice and Research*: Reactions and suggestions. *Consulting Psychology Journal, 65*(4), 278–283. https://doi.org/10.1037/a0035513

Schulman, J., Shaver, P., Coleman, R., Emrich, B., & Christie, R. (1973). Recipe for a jury. *Psychology Today, 37,* 37–44.

Schweitzer, N. J., & Saks, M. J. (2009). The gatekeeper effect: The impact of judges' admissibility decisions on the persuasiveness of expert testimony. *Psychology, Public Policy, and Law, 15*(1), 1–18. https://doi.org/10.1037/a0015290

Scobie, C., Semmler, C., & Proeve, M. (2019). Considering forensic science: Individual differences, opposing expert testimony and juror decision making. *Psychology, Crime & Law.* https://doi.org/10.1080/1068316X.2018.1488976

Seltzer, R. (2006). Scientific jury selection: Does it work? *Journal of Applied Social Psychology, 36*(10), 2417–2435. https://doi.org/10.1111/j.0021-9029.2006.00110.x

Semerdjian, D., & Mulligan, J. (2019, Winter). Jury selection: The often-overlooked make-it-or-break-it phase of a trial. *The Brief (American Bar Association), 48*(2), 10–17.

Shelton, S. T. (2006). Jury decision making: Using group theory to improve deliberation. *Politics & Policy, 34*(4), 706–725. https://doi.org/10.1111/j.1747-1346.2006.00037.x

Smith, L. J., & Malandro, L. A. (1985). *Courtroom communication strategies.* Kluwer.

Solnik, C. (2006, March 12). Mock juries offer a trial run for savvy lawyers. *St. Charles County Business Record.*

Spiecker, S. C., & Worthington, D. L. (2003). The influence of opening statement/closing argument organizational strategy on juror verdict and damage awards. *Law and Human Behavior, 27*(4), 437–456. https://doi.org/10.1023/A:1024041201605

Spier, K. E., & Prescott, J. J. (2019). Contracting on litigation. *The RAND Journal of Economics, 50*(2), 391–417. https://doi.org/10.1111/1756-2171.12274

Stored Communications Act, 18 U.S.C. §§ 2701–2712 (1986). https://en.wikipedia.org/wiki/Stored_Communications_Act

Strier, F. (1999). Whither trial consulting? Issues and projections. *Law and Human Behavior, 23*(1), 93–115. https://doi.org/10.1023/A:1022378824280

Swanepoel, M. (2010). Ethical decision-making in forensic psychology. *Koers, 75*(4), 851–872. https://doi.org/10.4102/koers.v75i4.110

Tabak, S. J., Klettke, B., & Knight, T. (2014). Simulated jury decision making in online focus groups. *Qualitative Research Journal, 13*(1), 102–113. https://doi.org/10.1108/14439881311314667

Taft, L. (2000). Apology subverted: The commodification of apology. *Yale Law Journal, 109*(5), 1135–1160. https://doi.org/10.2307/797485

Tanick, M. H., & Ayling, T. J. (1996). Alternative dispute resolution by apology: Settlement by saying "I'm sorry." *Hennepin Lawyer, 65*, 22.

Temme, L. (2019, August 27). *Social media use by juries: Is there any way to stop it?* https://blogs.findlaw.com/technologist/2019/08/social-media-use-by-juries-is-there-any-way-to-stop-it.html

Thies, D. (2013, April). New supreme court rule on juror questions presents opportunities for trial lawyers. *Illinois State Bar Association.*

Thornton, G. C., III, Eurich, T. L., & Johnson, R. (2009). Industrial/organizational psychologists as expert witnesses in employment discrimination litigation: Descriptions and prescriptions. *The Psychologist Manager Journal, 12*(3), 187–203. https://doi.org/10.1080/10887150903103448

Thornton, M. (2002). *Law and popular culture: Engendering legal vertigo.* Cavendish Publishing.

Townson, C. (2016). *Can I get a witness? Differences in juror perceptions and behavior across source type* (Publication No. 10156528) [Master's thesis, University of Delaware]. ProQuest Dissertations and Theses Global.

Trasatti, M. A., & Horevay, A. C. (2013). Litigation and social media: Using social media to your advantage at every step of the trial. *FDCC Quarterly, 63*, 252–278.

United States v. Tsarnaev, 945 F. Supp. 2d 230 (D. Mass. 2013).

United States v. Tsarnaev, 968 F.3d 24 (1st Cir. 2020).

United States v. Windsor, 570 U.S. 744 (2013).

U.S. Const. amend. I–X.

U.S. Const. amend. VI.

U.S. Const. art. III, § 2.

USLegal.com. (n.d.). *Weight of evidence law and legal definition.* https://definitions.uslegal.com/w/weight-of-evidence/

Vinson, K. V., Costanzo, M. A., & Berger, D. E. (2008). Predictors of verdict and punitive damages in high-stakes civil litigation. *Behavioral Sciences & the Law, 26*(2), 167–186. https://doi.org/10.1002/bsl.807

Wagstaff, T. W. (1989). Witness preparation. *University of Missouri Kansas City Law Review, 57*, 763–768.

Wallace, S. (2009). The internet infects the courtroom. *Judicature, 93*, 138–139.

Warger v. Shauers, 574 U.S. 40 (2014).

Wechsler, H. J., Kehn, A., Wise, R. A., & Cramer, R. J. (2015). Attorney beliefs concerning scientific evidence and expert witness credibility. *International Journal of Law and Psychiatry, 41*, 58–66. https://doi.org/10.1016/j.ijlp.2015.03.008

Wiener, R. L., Krauss, D. A., & Lieberman, J. D. (2011). Mock jury research: Where do we go from here? *Behavioral Sciences & the Law, 29*(3), 467–479. https://doi.org/10.1002/bsl.989

Wiggins v. Smith, 539 U.S. 510 (2003).

Wilford, M. M., Van Horn, M. C., Penrod, S. D., & Greathouse, S. M. (2018). Not separate but equal? The impact of multiple-defendant trials on juror decision-making. *Psychology, Crime & Law, 24*(1), 14–37. https://doi.org/10.1080/1068316X.2017.1351969

Wilson, T. (2019). The promise of behavioral economics for understanding decision-making in the court. *Criminology & Public Policy, 18*(4), 785–805. https://doi.org/10.1111/1745-9133.12461

Wingate, P. H., & Thornton, G. C., III. (2004). Industrial/organizational psychology and the federal judiciary: Expert witness testimony and the Daubert standards. *Law and Human Behavior, 28*(1), 97–114. https://doi.org/10.1023/B:LAHU.0000015005.29504.14

Woody, R. H. (2009). Ethical considerations of multiple roles in forensic services. *Ethics & Behavior, 19*(1), 79–87. https://doi.org/10.1080/10508420802623690

Wrightsman, L. S., & Heili, A. (1992). *Measuring bias in civil trials* [Unpublished manuscript]. Department of Psychology, University of Kansas.

Yates v. State of Texas, 171 S.W. 3d 215 (2005).

Zuckerman, M., DePaulo, B. M., & Rosenthal, R. (1981). Verbal and nonverbal communication of deception. In L. Berkowitz (Ed.), *Advances in experimental social psychology* (Vol. 14, pp. 1–59). Academic Press.

Index

About the Authors

Jay M. Finkelman, PhD, is a professor of industrial–organizational psychology at The Chicago School of Professional Psychology, Southern California Campuses. Previously, he served as vice president for academic affairs and department chair for the Business Psychology Department; senior vice president and general manager for Kelly Services in the human resource management and staffing industry; vice president in charge of marketing for Walt Disney television; and station manager of KTVU Television Channel 2 in San Francisco.

Dr. Finkelman serves as consultant and expert witness in employment, staffing, and human resources management and has had hundreds of retentions and depositions and testified at trial as an expert in employment practices. He has authored over 124 publications and coauthored four books, including *Neurodiversity Within a Divided Nation: The Nerve to Unite* (2019) and *The Psychologist Manager: Success Models for Psychologists in Executive Positions* (2013). Dr. Finkelman holds Diplomates from the American Board of Professional Psychology, in Organizational and Business Consulting Psychology, and in Forensic Psychology. He is a Fellow of the American Psychological Association, is a licensed psychologist in California and New York, and is listed in the National Register of Health Service Providers in Psychology.

Linda Gomberg, JD, PhD, has been a California attorney for over 4 decades. She has taught at every level from middle school in Evanston, Illinois, through law school in Southern California, while earning master's degrees in English and psychology. Most recently, after earning her PhD in psychology with an emphasis in media, Dr. Gomberg has taught as core faculty in and interim chair of the forensic psychology program at The Chicago School of Professional Psychology in Southern California; and she also served as the institutional review board chair for 5 years. She is the author of *Forensic Psychology 101* (2018) and has authored or coauthored several articles and a book chapter (with Carolyn Sachs, MPH, MD) in *Intimate Partner Violence: A Health-Based Perspective* on domestic violence. Aside from writing about and presenting on domestic violence, Dr. Gomberg has presented on other aspects of law and psychology for various organizations and continuing education. Among those were Licensed Masters in Family Therapy, CETYS (University in Northern Mexico) students, and Osher Lifelong Learning Institute. Through the American Psychological Association's (APA's) Division 46 (Society for Media Psychology and Technology), Linda Gomberg has twice presented at the APA Annual Convention and served as that division's conference cochair and ethics committee chair.